Jan Gralle | Vibe Skytte

111 Places
in Copenhagen
That You
Shouldn't
Miss

Photographs by Kurt Rodahl Hoppe

T0352124

emons:

© Emons Verlag GmbH

All rights reserved

Photographs by © Kurt Rodahl Hoppe, except:

ch. 13: Maija Heigaard; ch. 24: Bjørn Nørgaard/copydanbilleder.dk;

ch. 59 (top), 60, 65, 72, 90, 93, 98: Malte Oswaldo Trap Pedersen;

ch. 59 (bottom): iStock; ch. 64: Helene Høyer Mikkelse;

ch. 75 (bottom): CREO ARKITEKTER A/S. "Det genmodificerede paradis";

ch. 82: KVUC/Esben Salling; ch. 97: Irina Boersma

Chapters 44 and 83 were written in collaboration

with Morten Lander Anderse of østerbrobyvandring.dk.

Title of original edition: 111 steder i København som du skal se

© Bogforlaget Frydenlund

© Cover motif: private

Translated from the Danish by Kate Driscoll

Layout: Eva Kraskes, based on a design

by Lübbeke | Naumann | Thoben

Maps: altancicek.design, www.altancicek.de

Basic cartographical information from Openstreetmap,

© OpenStreetMap-Mitwirkende, ODbL

Printing and binding: Lensing Druck GmbH & Co. KG,

Feldbachacker 16, 44149 Dortmund

Printed in Germany 2019

ISBN 978-3-7408-0580-7

First edition

Did you enjoy this guidebook? Would you like to see more?
Join us in uncovering new places around the world on:
www.111places.com

Foreword

Which places in Copenhagen do you simply have to see? Are they the places where you have to queue up – like *The Little Mermaid* or the Round Tower? Or are they the hidden areas, easy to miss because they aren't listed as great attractions? We firmly believe it's the latter. This book focuses on 111 places in the capital region that you may not notice: the different, special and forgotten sights.

Copenhagen is an outdoors kind of city. This may seem strange since it's dark for most of the winter, and wind and rain are all too frequent during any season. But perhaps that's why Copenhageners take any opportunity to go out into the city or into nature. With the smallest ray of sunshine, everyone charges out to squares and pavements – or to the sea. It's hard to find a café that doesn't have outdoor seating, and even though we sit under heating lamps with freezing toes, wrapped in blankets over our coats and mittens, wild horses couldn't drag us inside away from the sunshine. This is also reflected in more than half of the sites mentioned in this book.

Copenhagen is also a city on the waterfront. A number of the chosen spots are therefore close to the harbour, the canals or the sea.

Choosing and writing about the 111 places has been a thoroughly enjoyable process. It has opened our eyes to new houses, parks and museums that even we – Copenhageners born and raised – didn't know, and it has helped us find new experiences in places we thought we knew.

We would like to thank all the visitors to our Facebook page '111 steder' who made suggestions and gave feedback on the chosen places.

Jan Gralle and Vibe Skytte

111 Places

1 Ågade Bridge
Distinctive and development-oriented design

41,200 on Kalvebod Brygge, 53,700 on Åboulevard/Ågade and 73,000 on Lyngbyvej. That's the daily number of cars on the three busiest roads leading into Copenhagen (2014).

Ågade's heavy traffic was an obstacle when building the Green Path from Lyngbyvej to Valby, allowing pedestrians and cyclists to go across town on a car-free and picturesque path. The solution was to elevate the path and lead it over the busy road via the 65-metre-long Åbuen, or Ågade Bridge.

Åbuen required unique engineering. It's built like an aeroplane wing and is supported on one side of a curved tube that goes through a series of tension rods. The engineering firm NIRAS was responsible for calculating the construction, and they were told not to change the project design drawings of architectural firm Dissing+Weitling. One of the engineers described it as a 'distinctive and development-oriented design', and it certainly wasn't easy – but they succeeded.

The arch was welded together as components in Poland, sent to England to be bent to the right curvature, and then sent back to Poland to be welded together into two parts that were sent to Åboulevarden and welded together into one. The various parts of the bridge were lifted into place over two days in Easter 2008, on a rare occasion when Ågade was closed to general traffic. The bridge was opened in June of that year, and since then it has been used by an average of 5,500 cyclists a day.

From Åbuen and the ramps up to it, you get a great view of the surrounding buildings, including the nursery school Stenurten, which is made mainly of recycled materials, and which serves organic meals that are – as per their own claim – 'of high culinary quality'. In addition to running across Åbuen, the Green Path goes past Superkilen (see ch. 100) and Nørrebroparken, along the University Gardens (see ch. 109) and into the distinctive landscape of Solbjerg Plads (see ch. 93).

Address Åbuen, 2200 Copenhagen N and 1958 Frederiksberg C | Getting there Bus 68 or Metro M 3 to Nuuks Plads | Tip The Green Path is roughly nine kilometres long and runs from Lyngbyvej in the north of Nørrebro and Frederiksberg to Valby in the west – much of its course follows a former railway route. There's currently about 58 kilometres of cycle routes in Copenhagen, and the plan is for that number to reach 115 kilometres by 2025.

2 — The Airplane Grill

Plane spotting for everyone

A female cyclist turns down the small lane which constitutes the last part of Amager Landevej. At the bottom of this cul-de-sac is a fence. She stops, takes off her helmet, finds a bottle of water in her bag and looks over the fence.

A group of pre-schoolers on a field trip sit up against the fence, eating packed lunches and chatting loudly: 'Here comes another one,' 'Wow, that's a big one' and 'It's so loud!'

Next to them are some workmen on their lunch break, and grandparents taking their grandchildren on a little excursion stand in line to order chips, burgers or soft serve ice cream. Once they've got their food, they walk up the small hill where there are benches and parasols, and they look over the fence.

This isn't just any old fast food stand; this is Flyvergrillen (The Airplane Grill), and from here you get the best view of the planes coming into and going out of Copenhagen Airport. SAS, easyJet, Lufthansa and KLM planes come and go regularly, and if you're there at the right time, you can see the jumbo jet from Thai Airways, which always draws a comment.

The number of visitors here is testament to the fact that this place appeals to children of all ages. There's room for both enthusiastic plane spotters, who stand about with their notepads and write down plane types and sizes and the number of landings, and for amateurs who are simply fascinated by seeing these enormous machines up close. On a sunny day, you can spend hours here just watching the planes take off and land, and if some children struggle to keep themselves occupied with the planes, they can go and play in the adjacent playground.

It helps that the grill serves all the classic Danish favourites, such as soft drinks in various rather toxic colours, chocolate milk, french fries, hot dogs and cheese toasties, as well as more fancy drinks, such as chai lattes.

Address Amager Landevej 290, 2770 Kastrup, www.flyver-grillen.dk | Getting there
Bus 34, 35 to Tømmerup Stationsvej | Hours Daily from 10.30am, closing times vary by
season, from between 5.30pm and 9.30pm | Tip From Vilhelm Lauritzens Allé 2 (a side
street off Amager Landevej) you can take a peek at the airport's VIP terminal from 1939, a
functionalist masterpiece by Vilhelm Lauritzen. It's here that the Danish Royal Family wait
for their flights. Unfortunately, it's closed to the public, so you'll have to admire it from afar.

3 Bakkehusmusee

A reminder of the cultural elite of the Golden Age

In the 18th century, Bakkehuset (The Hill House) was an inn just outside Copenhagen. After being bought by Kamma and Knud Lyne Rahbek in 1802, it became a central meeting place for Copenhagen's cultural elite, a status it retained until their deaths in 1829 and 1830, respectively. Knud Lyne Rahbek was professor and later chancellor of the University of Copenhagen, a board member of the Royal Theatre, editor of a number of journals and a prolific author following the rational and moral tradition of the late 18th century. Kamma Rahbek was a keen observer of trends, not least of romanticism, and she exchanged countless letters with the literary and cultural elite of the time.

The house itself may not look like much, and it's hard to imagine that the spot once overlooked all of historical Copenhagen and the sea around it. Yet much has been done to recreate the interiors of the house that once played host to informal gatherings of the movers and shakers of the Danish Golden Age, such as poet Adam Oehlenschläger, physicist H. C. Ørsted, pastor and poet N. F. S. Grundtvig and – not least – a young Hans Christian Andersen.

Bakkehusmuseet opened in 1925 under the name The Rahbek Museum, but rooms dedicated to Oehlenschläger and author Johannes Ewald were added later, and these rooms can still be viewed along with the Rahbeks' kitchen, library and numerous elegant studies and parlours.

The Municipality of Frederiksberg runs the museum and arranges special exhibitions, concerts and various activities for children. Even when not attending an event, the museum is well worth a visit. You're instantly transported back in time as you walk among fine oil paintings, dark wooden furniture and Empire-style curtains, while the worn desks and display cases full of books and letters impress upon you that great works of literature were written and inspired here.

Address Rahbeks Allé 23, 1801 Frederiksberg C, www.bakkehusmuseet.dk | Getting there Bus 18, 26 to Kammasvej | Hours Spring/summer: Tue–Sun 11am–5pm; autumn/winter: Wed–Sun 11am–4pm. The garden is always accessible. | Tip Søndermarken park is not far away, and during summer the museum offers tours on Sundays at 3pm. If you go from the entrance closest to the museum and walk diagonally across the park towards Roskildevej, you'll encounter the Norwegian Cabin and its garden, inspired by the landscape of the Norwegian mountains.

4_ The Banana House

A journeyman's house in Christiania

Christiania is world famous for being an area where anything can happen, with its extensive and obvious sale of hash, green ramparts and historic buildings such as Den grå Hal (the Grey Hall), Den grønne Hal (the Green Hall) and Mælkebøtten (the Dandelion), old military buildings for which the Christianites have found new purposes. Other buildings are newer and built with a great deal of imagination. One example is the Banana House, which was built by journeyman carpenters and is used as their residence as well as being a contact point for people who require their services.

A journeyman is a trained craftsman who travels and works various jobs around the world, a tradition dating back to the Middle Ages and known as 'going on the *Walz*'. Young craftsmen would travel in order to become more skilful by working for different master craftsmen, who would in turn provide room and board for no longer than six months. This tradition was widespread in Denmark until around the turn of the last century, and still exists, chiefly among carpenters in Germany and Switzerland. Journeyman carpenters are easy to spot due to their characteristic attire: a broad-brimmed hat, a double-breasted jacket and velvet waistcoat with an abundance of buttons, a white collarless shirt, black tie, bell-bottom trousers and a walking stick.

This isn't an outfit that lends itself well to modern carpentry, and the Banana House is built using traditional tools and largely without the use of nails. The journeymen started visiting Christiania in the early 1980s, partly because their work ethic harmonised so well with the free town's building principles of creative and alternative solutions and recycled materials. Christiania also offered many speciality jobs, and the journeymen could work for room, board and a small fee. The lodgings were, however, rather impractical (or perhaps too alternative) for the journeymen, so they built their own house in 1985. It takes its name from its shape seen from above.

Address Christiania, Bådsmandsstræde 43, 1407 Copenhagen K (on the bank behind Mælkebøtten), www.christiania.org | Getting there Bus 31, 37 or Metro M 1, M 2 to Christianshavn | Hours If there are journeymen carpenters in the house, it's usually possible to take a look inside | Tip Below the ramparts there is a bridge over the water to Amager and Kløvermarken.

5 BaNanna Park

Children flourish in a place where nothing would grow

A climbing wall, hopscotch, football, table tennis, a slide, swings, ball cage, running track and nets for street basketball – BaNanna Park has everything an inner-city kid could desire. Furthermore, there are the two banana-shaped earth banks, one of them with a yellow sports covering. It was once shiny and new, but now the yellow covering is worn down in many places, making the banana look somewhat overripe. That's not a bad thing, however, it's simply a sign that it's frequently used – perhaps as a spot for watching football or for running for safety during a game of tag.

The mural on the end wall reinforces the fact that you're in child territory now, as you're greeted by a long line of Danish children's TV characters, as well as Kermit, the Moomins and the residents of Fraggle Rock.

The little park in Nannasgade opened in 2010, before which it had been an abandoned lot, used as an unofficial playground for some years. Although the ground had been poisoned by an oil refinery that previously inhabited the spot, this did not stop the local school children who lived far away from real playgrounds and parks and therefore took what they could get.

Investors were getting ready to build on the lot in 2004, when the locals started a petition against the construction. The City heard their complaints and bought the lot, cleaned it up and started planning a new park in collaboration with neighbouring schools and residents. So now it's a lot more fun to be a kid in this inner-city neighbourhood. Outer Nørrebro and the neighbouring area of Nordvest are going through a transformation. Twenty years ago, they were on the outskirts of trendy Copenhagen, and the people living there were mostly welfare recipients. Today these two neighbourhoods are changing rapidly, with art galleries, popular restaurants and interesting shops popping up all over. The residents also represent a more diverse group than they did earlier.

Address Nannasgade 4, 2200 Copenhagen N | Getting there Bus 4A, 5C, 250S, 350S, 12, Metro M 3 or S-train F to Nørrebro; bus 5C to Stefansgade; bus 6A to Ægirsgade | Tip Buy a cup of coffee and walk past Odinsgade, where you can sip your coffee in Odin's Pocket, the first of many 'pocket parks' in Copenhagen.

6 Battery Sixtus

Where the sovereign flag greets soldiers and civilians alike

Can you really live next to a military base? Shouldn't they be sealed off with barbed wire, guards and surveillance cameras designed to keep intruders out?

Perhaps in some places, but not on Holmen. For several centuries the navy had its dockyard here, but now all that remains are the personnel service, the engineering school, the diving school and the officer candidate school, which occupy the north-eastern tip of the man-made island. Next door to these buildings lie a number of houseboats with an enviable view of the harbour to the west and the old ramparts to the east. All that the rest of us can do is console ourselves with the fact that most houseboats are quite small, so while the view may be spectacular, things probably get rather cramped!

When visiting Holmen, you're free to enter the grounds, as that's the only way of getting to the frigate *Peder Skram*, which was in use during the Cold War but now serves as a museum. This is also the way to Battery Sixtus, where the sovereign flag of Denmark has flown since 1788, when it was moved here from Kastellet (the Citadel). Naval officers raise the flag every day at dawn and lower it at night – either at sundown or 8pm, whichever comes first. The navy is also responsible for firing salutes from the cannon when foreign navies make official visits or on special occasions such as royal births. As such, the cannon has been in frequent use since 1999, when the first of Queen Margrethe's eight grandchildren was born.

In 2018, the Danish Parliament decided to move the navy away from its historical place on Holmen, but no final decision has been made as of yet. And with navy or not, Holmen is always worth a visit, especially on calm sunny days, when the sunlight sparkles in the water of the harbour basin. On such days, there is a special atmosphere of tranquility to the old docks, and it is a treat for young and old alike to stroll along here, sensing the presence of history.

Address Søværnets Officersskole, H. C. Sneedorffs Allé 3 and Batteriet Sixtus, 1439 Copenhagen K | **Getting there** Bus 2A to Fabrikmestervej | **Tip** You can also walk past the Central Guardhouse from 1745 (the house with the turret and crown) and the Masting Sheer from 1748, once used to mount masts on ships.

7 — Bellevue Beach

A touch of the Riviera – clothing optional

Bellevue Beach and the internationally renowned Danish architect Arne Jacobsen go hand in hand, as he is responsible for much of its most striking architecture. Influences from the Bauhaus movement and Le Corbusier are also evident, and you may feel as if you've been transported to the French Riviera when looking at the 1930s'-style white apartment buildings and bathing cabins. On a typical cold and grey day, you might want to skip the swim and instead combine your visit to the beach with a walk in the nearby Deer Park (Dyrehaven), and in the summer, you can swing by the amusement park Bakken, which may also be part of Bellevue's appeal. Roughly half a million people visit the beach each year, despite its relatively small size. Long known as 'the flypaper', the beach itself is approximately 700 metres long and only 20 to 40 metres wide, but there are also changing rooms, jetties and a large grassy area, where there is normally room to sit.

The beach is also popular among those who prefer to bathe *au naturel*, and the northernmost part of the beach in particular is frequented by nude bathers. Significantly more men come here than women, and the beach is internationally known as one of Copenhagen's best 'gay beaches', which may explain some of its popularity.

The excellent train connections from central Copenhagen have been transporting people to the Deer Park, the Bakken amusement park and the Sanatorium since the 1860s. Very little of the spa remains today, but it was designed by another famous architect, Gottlieb Bindesbøll, in the 1840s.

Bellevue – including the changing area and lifeguard towers – were Arne Jacobsen's first big assignment, and he also spearheaded the building of the Bella Vista apartments and the Bellevue Theatre. Years later, in the 1940s, he was responsible for a housing project nearby and built a house for himself on Strandvejen 413. Both the house and its garden have been preserved as they were when Jacobsen died in 1971, and they can be viewed on special occasions.

Address Strandvejen 340, 2930 Klampenborg, www.bellevuestrandbad.dk | Getting there S-train C to Klampenborg; bus 23 to Bellevue | Tip The former fishing village Taarbæk, just north of Bellevue, has a beach that's well suited for children, and where the locals bathe off the piers.

8 Bernstorffs Palæ
From royal court to court of law

You can find two opulent buildings in Bredgade, the likes of which you won't find elsewhere in Copenhagen. Dehns Palæ and Bernstorfs Palæ are named after their first owners, F. L. Dehn and J. H. E. Bernstorf, who both served as ministers under the absolute monarch Frederik V (1723–1766).

The mansions were built to form an axis with the Marble Church and the buildings that would later become Amalienborg Palace. They were designed in the rococo style of the day, and both were outfitted with impressive staircases. Bernstorffs Palæ is now home to the Eastern High Court of Denmark, and is worth a visit for the staircase alone, which is a unique example of a Danish rococo interior. Four magnificent French tapestries were made for the mansion but were later sold off, and they – along with rococo furniture from the house – can now be seen at the Metropolitan Museum of Art in New York.

One of the owners of the mansion was the Greek King George I (1845–1913). He was a Danish prince, son of Queen Louise (see ch. 84), and was elected king of Greece in 1863, with the backing of the major European powers of the time. George I reigned for almost 50 years, but would periodically return to Denmark and was therefore in need of a suitable residence. He only occupied the ground floor, and in his absence he would allow the remainder of the mansion to be used for various purposes. When Christiansborg Palace burnt down in 1884, for example, he allowed the Supreme Court to move into one of the parlours. He also lent parts of the mansion to another Danish prince, Charles, who lived there with his family until he became king of the newly independent Norway in 1905.

After King George's death, the palace was no longer home to royalty. It was sold to a private company and then to an insurance brokers, who now rent it out to the High Court.

Address Bredgade 42, 1260 Copenhagen K, www.domstol.dk/oestrelandsret | Getting there Bus 23 to Dronningens Tværgade / Odd Fellow Palæet; Metro M 3 to Marmorkirken | Hours Mon–Fri 8.30am–3pm, closed in July | Tip If you wish to look inside, all court cases are usually open to the public, unless the judge has decided otherwise.

9 The Bicycle Snake

The bridge just for cyclists, that's used by everyone

In the summer of 2014, the bridge known as the Bicycle Snake (or Bicycle Tube) was opened, meaning that cyclists no longer had to haul their bicycles up and down flights of stairs if they wanted to cross the Bryggebro Bridge connecting Amager and Zealand. This was a welcome development indeed! The Bicycle Snake cost 32 million DKK to build, is 230 metres long and 4 metres wide and was designed by the firm Dissing+Weitling Architecture, an offshoot of renowned architect Arne Jacobsen's studio, which was also known for its minimalist aesthetic. The firm is also responsible for a number of bridges in Denmark, such as the Great Belt Bridge (connecting Zealand and Funen) and the Øresund Bridge (connecting Denmark and Sweden), as well as bridges and other buildings in Scotland, Sweden and South Africa, to name a few, so they're experienced to say the least.

However, there was one thing that they didn't expect from the bridge, which is only meant to be used by cyclists: pedestrians love it. This forbidden love is much to the chagrin of the cyclists who routinely have to dodge wheelchair users, skateboarders, rollerbladers, parents with prams and strollers, and others who wish to avoid the stairs leading to the waterfront.

The steel railings twist rather haphazardly, which must annoy the perfectionistic architects. The gentle swings of the bridge itself are there by design, however. The offset entrance and exit allow for a better flow when crossing the bridge, making it perfect for cyclists – that is if they keep their eyes open for obstructions. In addition to the pedestrians, cyclists must also be on the lookout for people who flout the law against diving off the bridge, not to mention the danger of diving at the bridge's highest point, where it rises six metres above the surface. People are actively encouraged to bathe in the appropriate parts of the harbour, and if you must walk across the Bicycle Snake, do please be aware of the cyclists.

Address Kalvebod Brygge 59, 1561 Copenhagen V, or via Bryggebroen from Islands Brygge 32, 2300 Copenhagen S | Getting there Bus 10 or S-train A, B, Bx, C, E, H to Dybbølsbro | Tip The Fisketorvet shopping centre has a great number of different shops, a large cinema, cash machines, cafés, restaurants and a pharmacy (www.fisketorvet.dk).

10__Bispebjerg Hill
Where art meets architecture

On Bispebjerg Hill (Bispebjerg Bakke), a cul-de-sac behind Bispebjerg Hospital, a house snakes up and down and back and forth through the terrain. The building is the brainchild of artist and sculptor Bjørn Nørgaard, with help from a team of architects and engineers. It was an ambitious project from the start, and its purpose was to show that good, solid craftsmanship is still alive and well in Denmark.

In 1997, house painter Klaus Bonde Larsen was chairman of the Craftsmen's Association and member of a government committee for the protection of traditional craftsmanship, of which artist Bjørn Nørgaard was also a member. The two men knew each other through a project that Nørgaard had worked on for the Royal Copenhagen Shooting Society (see ch. 89), designing and creating one of the artful shooting targets that new members of the society were to present upon their admission. It was Nørgaard and Larsen's acquaintance which led to the development on Bispebjerg Hill, on a plot of land formerly housing the plant nursery for the Municipality of Copenhagen Gardening Department.

The construction of 11 houses (containing 135 apartments) was completed in 2006, after several compromises on cost and the level of quality that could be afforded, and after a large donation from the philanthropic fund Realdania. The houses are separated by a kind of gate, a reference to the traditional brick city blocks of the Nordvest neighbourhood, the home of the house snake and where Nørgaard himself grew up. The apartments are between 85 and 250 square metres in size and cost between 10,000 and 20,000 DKK per month to rent. Recently one of the largest apartments was up for rent: the one in the very head of the snake, with 254 square metres divided over three floors. The listing mentioned no specific price, but promised an 'attractive rent to be arranged'. Whatever was arranged was probably not exactly cheap, but perhaps a small price to pay to live in a place like no other!

Address Bispebjerg Bakke 18A-23F, 2400 Copenhagen NV, www.bispebjergbakke.dk | Getting there Bus 6A to Bispebjerg Hospital, 43 to Gribskovvej; S-train B, Bx to Emdrup | Tip The building overlooks a park called Lersøparken, where you can get on the Green Path – a foot and bicycle path which takes you to Nørrebro and Frederiksberg.

11__ The Blackberries in Kløvermarke

Pick them yourself and enjoy the view

The brambles grow wildly and freely here on the edge of Kløver-marken, a common next to the long-abandoned Amager railway and long line of allotments, as they have done for generations. As the thorny vines die and lie on top of each other, new vines grow over them, and in several places they have become high, impenetrable thickets, and you may need very long arms to get at the berries.

If you've come out here, you'll notice the incredible view. The common became listed in 2011 because it was deemed important to preserve it as a recreational area, and because there's a view of the Christianshavn ramparts and the adjoining demarcation area, as well as many of the city's towers and spires as a backdrop.

The tracks from the Amager railway are still there, for the most part. The railway was opened in 1907 and was used to transport both passengers and goods. In the first few years it was used to remove waste from the city outhouses, giving the island its somewhat unfor-tunate yet tenacious nickname 'Shit Island'. The railway was officially closed in 1975, but the society for the Friends of the Amager Rail-way still have great plans for it. They arrange occasional rides on the tracks, something that they would like to do more. That dream clashes with the City's plans to build a super bicycle path along the tracks, which will then join up with the other super paths in Copenhagen.

There is no trace left of the large refugee camps which were es-tablished in Kløvermarken after the Second World War. In Novem-ber 1945, the first refugees were housed in Swedish wooden houses, which had been bought for that purpose, and by August 1946, there were almost 18,000 refugees living behind the barbed wire that sur-rounded Kløvermarken, many of them living in tents. They were gone by the summer of 1949, and Kløvermarken became the sports ground that it is today.

Address Prags Boulevard / Uplandsgade, 2300 Copenhagen S | Getting there Bus 37 to
Ved Amagerbanen; bus 31 to Holmbladsgade / Strandlodsvej, then follow the tracks along
Kløvermarken | Tip From Kløvermarksvej 70 you can walk or bike across the Christianshavn
ramparts to Christiania.

12 Bopa Plads
Named after sabotage – great for a cup of coffee

Just a short walk from the bustle of Østerbrogade you'll find Bopa Plads, well known to those on parental leave or other groups meeting up for a cup of coffee at the establishments Pixie and Bopa, which have café-style outdoor seating during the day and are lively bars in the evening.

The streets in this area of Østerbro are named after Danish towns, and when the neighbourhood was built up in the late 1800s, a small triangular plot was left over, which became Randers Square (named after a town in East Jutland). It had cramped blocks of apartment buildings on one side and large detached houses on the other, similar to the buildings on Rosenvænget (see ch. 87). Most of these houses now belong to the City, which has been turning them into childcare institutions as well as introducing traffic calming measures in the area.

In connection with the 50th anniversary of the liberation of Denmark in May 1945, Randers Plads was renamed Bopa Plads in honour of BOPA, the most powerful of the Danish resistance groups. The name BOPA stood for 'Bourgeois Partisans', but it was originally called Communist Partisans and its members were mainly communists and former volunteers from the Spanish Civil War. The name change was most likely an attempt to attract new members – in which case it succeeded, especially members with knowledge of the large factories which were often the targets of sabotage. The group was so effective that it was responsible for a third of the 843 registered acts of sabotage in Copenhagen, and for 60% of the damages suffered by the companies that cooperated with the Nazis.

Apart from the name, there is no reference to the group or the war. In fact, if you have children, you'll find one of the most peaceful playgrounds in the city, with its 'fruit playground' with large wooden fruit. While the children play, adults can try their hand at a game of boules next door.

Address Bopa Plads, 2100 Copenhagen Ø | Getting there Bus 1A to Århusgade or Gustav Adolfs Gade | Tip The beautiful Øbro-Hal swimming pool and spa is at the opposite end of Nøjsomhedsvej (teambade.kk.dk).

13_Brumleby
Monument – and desirable housing

Once in a blue moon, an apartment in Brumleby becomes available, but the residents are so fond of the area that they'd rather move around it several times than move out altogether. Not that you can blame them. Where else in Copenhagen would you find relatively cheap housing with small gardens and green communal areas in the middle of one of the most attractive parts of town? So although you can put your name down for an apartment, you're unlikely to be successful unless you already have an equally attractive apartment to offer up in trade.

This is, however, a far cry from the Brumleby of the 1960s, which was damp and run-down, with shared outhouses and apartments so small that most people lived there out of necessity and lack of options. The development was originally called The Medical Association's Residences, because it was built in the 1850s after a deadly outbreak of cholera in a seriously overpopulated Copenhagen. The cure for cholera was thought to be fresh air and good hygiene, which is why 'only' 20 people had to share an outhouse in Brumleby, unlike other parts of the city, where up to 60 people would have to share.

Between the houses were communal toilet and laundry facilities, as well as gardens belonging to some of the houses, which was practical for families with children. Despite the doctors' recommendations, however, the apartments remained as cramped as they were elsewhere in Copenhagen. Brumleby originally comprised 550 apartments, which became 220 apartments after a refurbishment in the 1990s.

After the Second World War, the area came to be seen as sociopolitically and architecturally significant, and the buildings were listed in 1959. When the City of Copenhagen took over Brumleby in 1966 they prepared for demolition. In the meantime, some young people and students had moved in, and they managed to save the buildings.

Address Brumleby, Østerbrogade, 2100 Copenhagen Ø | Getting there Bus 1A to Gustav Adolfs Gade; bus 1A, 14 or Metro M 3 to Trianglen | Tip Brumleby is right next to the Fælledparken commons, which often hosts large events such as the Whitsun Carnival, or where you can go for long walks and try out the many playgrounds.

14__ The Burial Ground for the Homeless

The only one of its kind in the world

Who remembers the homeless when they die? Who attends their funerals? Where are they even buried? Can you visit their graves and pay your respects? Yes, you can, at the Assistens Cemetery!

Since 2013, 75 square metres of the cemetery has been reserved for the homeless. Urns of deceased homeless people are interred here, and others from the homeless community can come here to mourn and remember their friends. At the gravesite is a little monument called *An angel among us*, created by artist and musician Leif Sylvester. An abundance of roses, tulips, lilies and pansies grow or lie around the bottom of the sculpture. It's practically a small garden, and it's tended by Captain Irishman and other members of the homeless community, who bring new flowers that have been thrown away by supermarkets or found in the city's rubbish bins each day.

The burial place was initiated by an association called Giv Din Hånd (Give Your Hand), and it's the only one of its kind in the world. The work began in 2011, when the 'memorial tree' for the homeless at Kultorvet was cut down. This was once a place where you could hang pictures of and poems dedicated to the deceased, because the City would bury the homeless wherever there was room or where the plots were cheap. It was therefore not possible to visit late homeless friends, as no one really knew where they were buried.

Fortunately, both the City and the parish took kindly to Giv Din Hånd's proposal to create a burial place for the homeless and others on the margins of society. They offered up the space on Assistens Cemetery, a beautifully landscaped green space which is as much a park as a burial space, and where luminaries such as poet H. C. Andersen is also buried. Now the homeless can finally be laid to rest properly, next to their friends, and have a place where they belong.

Address Section M, Assistens Kirkegård, 2200 Copenhagen N | Getting there Bus 18 to Jægersborggade; bus 68 or Metro M3 to Nuuks Plads | Hours Apr–Sept, daily 7am–10pm; Oct–Mar, daily 7am–7pm | Tip Although it was originally supposed to be a pauper's cemetery, many famous Danes are buried in Assistens Cemetery, including Søren Kierkegaard and Niels Bohr, as well as the famous American jazz musicians Ben Webster and Kenny Drew.

15__Bus 5C
Crosstown traffic

With about 20 million passengers each year, bus 5C serves the next highest number of people after Copenhagen Airport (29 million in 2017). They're both among the busiest in the Nordic countries, but this isn't good enough for the airport, which aims to serve 40 million people a year. This ambition is mercifully not shared by bus 5C (the C is for Cityline). If you take it during rush hour – where up to 45 buses run at once – you might feel like it serves 20 million passengers a day rather than per year. Since the bus goes along many of the busiest streets in Copenhagen, it takes quite a while to get anywhere because so many people get on and off at all stops, but if you're not in a hurry, you have a great opportunity to get a sense of urban life in Copenhagen.

In 2017, the new and current fleet of turquoise, segmented 5C buses was inaugurated, each bus modernised to run on biogas and fit in even more passengers, while making boarding and exiting easier with more doors. Each door serves as both exit and entrance, while most other Danish buses can only be boarded from the front.

The 5C runs right across town from the suburb of Herlev in the north-westernmost part of the Copenhagen municipality, to the airport in the southeast. It's the oldest route in the city and began as a tramline in 1903 – the last tram route to be taken out of commission in 1972. The route itself has varied over the years, but it has always gone through Nørrebro, the centre of town and Amager. It has no fixed timetable, but runs regularly around the clock, approximately every four minutes during the day and every 10 to 30 minutes in the evening and at night.

Bus 5C goes past quiet areas such as Husum Torv and Sundbyvester Plads, as well as busier stretches like Nørrebrogade and Amagerbrogade. In the centre of town, it takes you past Tivoli and the Carlsberg Glyptotek as well as the bombastic Police Headquarters, a prime example of Nordic classicism.

Address Between Husum Torv and Sundbyvester Plads (slightly fewer busses run between Husum Torv and Copenhagen Airport), www.moviatrafik.dk | **Tip** If you're going to the airport it's much faster to take the metro line M2.

16 Caritas Fountain

The Danish 'Manneken Pis' and his mother

The little urinating boy who is part of the group of figures on the Caritas Fountain is from 1608 (and therefore slightly older than his counterpart from Brussels, who was put up in 1619). He is placed quite high up, and most people pay him little notice. Perhaps they don't even see that water also sprays out of his mother's breasts; she is both pregnant and lactating, and she symbolises charity (in Latin: *caritas*), the greatest of the three theological virtues, along with faith and hope.

The fountain was originally a bronze-decorated well, and under the fountain there is a large reservoir. The well was placed in the middle of the square, because the only city hall was located where the pedestrian street Strøget now runs between the two squares, Gammeltorv and Nytorv.

In the past, Nytorv was the site of public executions and floggings well into the 18th century, while Gammeltorv was a market square until the early 20th century. The oldest Copenhageners can still very well remember the traders and their live chickens walking around the square.

The fountain has undergone numerous changes over the years. Caritas was originally at eye level for those who drew water from the well, but apparently that was too close for some people. In the early 18th century, a barrier was put up around the fountain and later it was raised onto a pedestal of Norwegian marble. In the mid-19th century, it was 'censored', and Caritas' nipples and the little boy's penis were plugged up. They were reopened in 1890, when winged dolphins were added and all traces of the well were removed.

In 2009, the group of figures was cleaned and re-gilded, but there are no plans to return it to its original height. One tradition remains, however, as gilded copper baubles are put in the fountain on royal birthdays, where they can bounce in the water streams in the top basin.

Address Gammeltorv, 1457 Copenhagen K | Getting there Bus 5C, 6A, 150S, 14, 184, 185; Metro M1, M2 or S-train A, B, Bx, C, E, H to Nørreport; bus 2A, 5C, 250S, 10, 23, 33 or Metro M3 to Rådhuspladsen | Tip Today there are very few outdoor or covered markets in Copenhagen. One example is the Torvehallerne, just by Nørreport Station.

17 __ The Chapel
in Holmen Church

A 17th-century church with real naval heroes

From the outside, the chapel may look like a kind of banquet hall, especially at night, when the large crystal chandeliers light up the 21 windows overlooking the canal, and you can hear the dulcet tones of a concert within. Yet it remains a hall for the dead, with coffins, memorial plaques and epitaphs, and below there is a crypt with small barred windows.

The church itself was built in 1619 as an anchor smithy, from which the anchors were sailed away on transport ships. When the smithy was converted into a church, it was therefore possible to sail in the coffins rather than have to carry them. The chapel and crypt were built between 1705 and 1706 in order for the church to make money from upper-class citizens who were willing to pay a little extra for a special spot for their coffins in the crypt and a memorial plaque in the chapel. In 1709, the first coffin was moved into its own little chapel. It contained the remains of Niels Juel (1629–1697), a Danish naval hero, who had fought in several wars against Sweden. Another great naval officer, Peter Wessel (1690–1720), was not afforded the same treatment. In Denmark, he is better known by his noble title, Tordenskiold, one of the greatest naval heroes of all time. He was responsible for several notable victories, as is stated on the sarcophagus in which his coffin was placed 100 years after his death. He had died in a duel, and was therefore prohibited by law from having a Christian funeral. The coffin containing his embalmed remains was taken to the chapel under cover of darkness in 1721 and placed in the crypt until the king, Frederik VI, could have him reinstated and moved into the chapel.

There are many other interesting coffins and memorial plaques to be seen in the chapel, and you can of course visit the church itself, which is well preserved with beautiful 17th-century decorations.

Address Holmens Kanal 21, 1060 Copenhagen K, www.holmenskirke.dk | Getting there Bus 23, 26 to Holmens Kirke; bus 2A, 31, 37 to Børsen; Metro M 3 to Gammel Strand; Hop On-Hop Off Boats (stromma.dk) and Canal Boats (havnerundfart.dk) dock at the church jetty | Hours Mon, Wed, Fri & Sat 10am–4pm, Tue & Thu 10am–3.30pm, Sun & holidays noon–4pm | Tip Børsen (the former stock exchange) with its Dragon Spire (where the tails of four dragons are intertwined) often hosts different events and exhibitions which allow you in for a peek at the interiors.

18__Christian's Church
The Theatre Church

Is God a performer? This might be the first thing to strike you upon entering Christian's Church. It's known colloquially as 'the theatre church' due to its unusual layout with many boxes facing the 'stage', or in this case, the pulpit.

This layout makes the church a prime example of a Protestant house of prayer, where the sermon is seen as the central and most important part of the service.

Copenhagen was teeming with Germans in the 18th century, not only those who came from the duchies of Schleswig and Holstein, which were part of the Danish-Norwegian kingdom at the time, but German merchants and craftsmen were also frequently seen in the city. They had their own congregations, such as St Peter's Church (see ch. 98), but also wanted one in Christianshavn. It was erected between 1755 and 1759 and was named Frederik's German Church after King Frederik V. The church was designed in the rococo style by Nicolai Eigtved (1701–1754), the Royal Building Master and man responsible for the Frederiksstaden district and Amalienborg Palace.

The German congregation diminished in the late 19th century due to increasing nationalist sentiment and the antagonism towards the Prussians following the Schleswig Wars in 1848–1850 and in 1864, when Denmark lost Schleswig and Holstein to Prussia. Many Germans chose to move from Denmark during this period. In 1886, the congregation ceased its activities and the church fell into disuse for 15 years.

In 1901, it became part of the Danish National Church and changed its name to Christian's Church to avoid confusion with Frederik's Church (The Marble Church).

The church also contains a crypt, which is well worth a visit, but do remember to be considerate of any mourners. The crypt has been in use for 250 years since the church was consecrated in 1759.

Address Strandgade 1, 1401 Copenhagen K | Getting there Bus 2A, 31, 37 or Harbour Bus 991, 992 to Knippelsbro | Hours Tue−Fri 10am−4pm | Tip Take a walk through Strandgade and have a look at the numerous 17th-century merchant's houses. Many famous Danes have lived in Strandgade, such as pastor and poet N. F. S. Grundtvig and naval hero Tordenskjold. There are memorial plaques on the façades or in courtyards.

19 __ Christianshavn Boat Rental and Café

Lunch on the Canal

Those who think of Christianshavn as just a bump in the road on the way from Amager to Zealand will never experience the quiet and intimate setting not found elsewhere in Copenhagen. Once you get away from the traffic on Torvegade and onto one of its six cross streets, a whole new world opens up: you're embraced by Christianshavn, and you'll quickly come to realise that this is a part of town like no other.

Christianshavn was founded by King Christian IV, who hired a Dutch city planner to draw up the neighbourhood – imagined by the king as an independent merchant town – with its artificial islands, little bridges and canals. It was soon incorporated into Copenhagen proper, but still holds a unique atmosphere, especially noticeable if you walk down one of the streets on either side of the canal. It's hard to say whether this feeling is due to the beautiful 17th-century houses, the cobblestone streets, the many trees, the abundance of parked bicycles or the water which surrounds and flows through all of Christianshavn. Perhaps it's the sum of all these parts.

Down by the boat rental and café, you can also feel the Christian-shavn calm as you walk down the steps to the old boat, which bobs in the canal. During summer, the café offers food and drink and there are often concerts. Heating lamps and blankets keep you warm on cold evenings and canopies shield you from the rain.

While you enjoy a drink, you can keep an eye on the water, where tour boats, kayaks and speed boats sail past in a steady procession. Should you get the urge to go out on the water, you can hire a row-ing boat and life jacket at the café – in fact, the boat rental opened in 1898, making it far older than the café, which is only from 1996.

If you come by in November or December you can warm yourself with a cup of their famous homemade mulled wine.

Address Overgaden Neden Vandet 29, 1414 Copenhagen K, baadudlejningen.dk, facebook.com/christianshavnsbaadudlejningogcafe | Getting there Bus 31, 37 or Metro M1, M2 to Christianshavn | Hours See the Facebook page – we recommend booking a table, especially at the weekend | Tip On the corner of Overgaden Oven Vandet and Torvegade you'll find the modernist building Lagkagehuset (The Layer Cake House), built in 1930. The name derives from the yellow and white striped façade, which makes it look like layers of whipped cream and custard.

20 _ The Circle Bridge

Room for reflection

The Circle Bridge (Cirkelbroen) is designed to make you think, and you're meant to slow down and reflect while crossing it – at least according to the Danish-Icelandic artist, Ólafur Elíasson, who designed it. For his part, the bridge makes him think of the masts of the fishing boats he saw as a child in Iceland. You are, however, free to interpret the bridge in any way you like; in interviews leading up to the opening of the bridge in August 2015, Elíasson said that if it made people think of harps, for example, that was fine by him.

It isn't entirely clear what the Circle Bridge is 'supposed to be'. In short, it can be described as five circular platforms of varying sizes, each resting on a slender pillar in the water and with a tall mast, which are fastened to the platforms with approximately 100 tensioned wires. A short ramp leads up to the bridge deck. The maritime inspiration is reflected in the details; for example, in the dark oiled wood used for the railings.

Above water it's a work of art, but below the surface it's a marvel of engineering. The engineers came up with a way of enabling the bridge to open easily and elegantly: two of the platforms float on top of a ballast tank containing approximately 100 cubic metres of air. The only disadvantage is that the bridge can't be opened when the water is frozen, but then again, it wouldn't need to!

Before the construction of the Circle Bridge, The Municipality of Copenhagen had long desired to build a continuous path for pedestrians and cyclists in Christianshavn, which would make everyday life much easier for the many bike commuters in the area. The wish, however, clashed with boat owners' desire to be able to sail in and out of the Christianshavn Canal without having to wait for bridges to open. The debate was at its most heated regarding the channel by the Paper Island, where most ships with masts sail. There, the problem was solved with a bridge guard, while you can open the Circle Bridge yourself or make arrangements in advance for it to be opened.

Address Christianshavn, 1411 Copenhagen K | Getting there Bus 2A, 31, 37 to Knippelsbro; bus 31, 37 or Metro M1, M2 to Christianshavn | Tip The Circle Bridge is part of the eastern harbour front promenade reaching from Knippelsbro over Islands Brygge to the Bryggebro Bridge (and the Bicycle Snake, see ch. 9).

21 — The Circle Line

Ride across town

If you want to experience a cross section of Copenhagen just outside the centre of town, you can take a trip on the S-train line F, the Circle Line (Ringbanen), which goes from Hellerup in the north to Ny Ellebjerg in the south – and back again, so not much of a circle, really.

The Circle Line includes much of Copenhagen's oldest S-train line, which was opened in 1934, when it connected Frederiksberg (which is why it's the F line), Vanløse, Nørrebro and Hellerup with Klampenborg, so the residents of the more densely populated areas could quickly get out to the forests and beaches of Northern Zealand (see ch. 7). These days, the F train only goes to Klampenborg on Friday and Saturday nights. Instead, it has become a popular commuter route, as it links together the various lines going from the city centre to the neighbouring municipalities.

If you take the train from Hellerup Station, you'll ride past big detached houses and gardens, as well as Mindelunden (the Memorial Grove) – a memorial for those members of the Resistance who were executed or died during the occupation of Denmark. After you reach Ryparken Station, industrial complexes, parks and allotments dominate the view. At Nørrebro Station, you can see directly into people's bedrooms and kitchens, because the Circle Line becomes an elevated railway until Grøndal Station, where there's a large residential area built between 1914 and 1928 by young architects who chose to build in styles closer to home rather than the popular European historical styles of the time. After Grøndal Station, you continue on through Frederiksberg and its large detached houses to Flintholm Station, which was meant to be one of the major traffic arteries, although it looks rather worn and empty outside rush hour. Once you've gone through Frederiksberg and Vanløse's lovely residential areas, you'll be met by large industrial areas currently undergoing major re-zoning.

Route Hellerup – Ryparken – Bispebjerg – Nørrebro – Fuglebakken – Grøndal – Flint-holm – KB Hallen – Ålholm – Danshøj – Vigerslev Allé – Ny Ellebjerg (and Klampen-borg – Ordrup – Charlottenlund on Friday and Saturday nights) | Getting there S-train F from one of the stops above | Tip It's a short walk from Hellerup Station to the most exclusive shops on Strandvejen.

22__The City Hall Garden
A myriad of details

There are photos from 1907 showing children playing in the City Hall Garden with their mothers or nannies. In other photos, you can see how the garden continued on through the gate to what is now H. C. Andersens Boulevard, and how it was full of children and prams. However, that's all in the past. In 1954, the boulevard was widened, leaving just one flowerbed behind, and there were hardly any children left in the area. Families had moved out of the city centre, and the garden behind the City Hall was all but forgotten.

When the City Hall celebrated its 100th anniversary in 2005, the garden was finally redone. It was returned as far as possible to its original symmetrical state, but now with added standing trellises.

In the middle of the garden is the Bear Fountain, depicting a bear catching the water in his mouth. It was sculpted by Joakim Skovgaard (1856–1933) and designed by Torvald Bindesbøll (1846–1908), both of them very prominent artists of their time. The fountain has been here since the garden was put in, but it was originally designed in 1888 for a competition to decorate Højbro Square (Højbro Plads). The winning entry was the equestrian statue of Bishop Absalon (founder of Copenhagen according to conventional wisdom), but the placement in the City Hall Garden really isn't a bad consolation prize for the little bear.

With its closed courtyard, the garden somewhat resembles an Italian Renaissance square. Yet it's difficult to pin a label on the rest of the City Hall building. It was designed by Martin Nyrop (1849–1921), who was inspired by different styles from many countries and decorated the building with a cornucopia of quirky ornamental details. As you sit on one of the benches in the garden, let your eyes drift and your mind be surprised by them. You should also note the bricks around you, unusual in that they're made from two types of clay – red and yellow – mixed together. This accounts for their beautiful varied shades.

Address Rådhuspladsen 1, 1550 Copenhagen V. Entrance through the side gates on H. C. Andersens Boulevard and Vester Voldgade | **Getting there** Bus 2A, 5C, 250S, 10, 23, 33 or Metro M3 to Rådhuspladsen | **Hours** Daily 9am–4pm, it may be closed on special occasions | **Tip** The Dragon Fountain on the City Hall Square was also created by Skovgaard and Bindesbøll. It depicts a bull fighting a serpent, legendary creatures from Nordic and Germanic legends, while small dragons spray water from the edge. The same kind of dragons as can be seen crawling up the City Hall were part of a larger surrounding basin.

23___The Climbing Wall in Sydhavne

Climb up Frederiksholm Church

Why not climb up a church tower? It's there after all, standing 18 metres tall, and who says it's only for church bells?

In 2014, the Frederiksholm Church in Sydhavnen (The South Harbour) opened its climbing wall. The wall isn't just there for fun, interest or exercise, though. The Reverend Helene Ferslev, who initiated the building of the climbing wall, explains on the church's website that:

'It's ok to feel like you're being challenged when you go to church. Faith is basically trust and hope, and with the climbing wall you can challenge your courage and your trust. The physical challenge brought by the wall is similar to way you feel on the inside when you have faith. If you want to believe, you have to be brave enough to let go of the earth in order to find answers and reason in something greater than yourself. Similarly, you quite literally leave the ground when you climb up and abseil down the church tower.'

The church has its own climbing events, e.g. for children taking confirmation classes, but anyone – children, young people, adults, companies – can book a time to go climbing all year round, unless it coincides with other activities. You can bring your own certified climbing instructor, but you'll always be assisted by someone from the church.

The wall is 144 square metres in total, stands at 15.6 metres tall and has approximately 400 climbing holds. There are six different ways to climb, adjusted for different age groups.

Close to the church you can find Karens Minde Kulturhus, a cultural centre housed in a lovely old building from the very beginning of the 19th century. Its café hosts communal eating every Thursday, always a cheap and social way to enjoy your dinner. The Kulturhus also hosts a variety of events such as concerts and pub quizzes.

Address Louis Pios Gade 8, 2450 Copenhagen SV, www.sydhavnsogn.dk/klatrevæg |
Getting there S-train A, E to Sjælør; bus 7A, 9A, 18, 23 to Mozarts Plads | Hours
1 Apr – 1 Oct | Tip Just around the corner are the Frem Allotments – houses built around
a little lake. It's an idyllic and alternative way of living in the city.

24 The Concert Church
A world of music in Nørrebro

Norbert Rodenkirchen puts his flute to his lips and lets its dulcet tones flow out into the audience. They're listening to the story of the Pied Piper of Hamelin, told to them through Rodenkirchen's melodies. The reverberations give clout to the sound and fill up the church, while the audience sips white wine or soft drinks bought at the bar. There are roughly 20 people in the Concert Church this Saturday afternoon, where Rodenkirchen is performing as part of the Copenhagen Renaissance Music Festival.

In a few hours, the church benches will be put away and the evening's entertainment (Urban Salsa Night – five and a half hours of Latin music and dancing) can begin.

Blågårds Church was deconsecrated in 2008 and has housed the Concert Church since 2009. In 2015, the organisation responsible for the Concert Church bought the building with financial support from a number of foundations.

The programme includes all types of music because, as they state on their website, the purpose is to present the highest quality music of any genre that broadens, challenges and blows your mind.

With its location in inner Nørrebro, just off the lovely (although sometimes turbulent) Blågårds Square (Blågårds Plads), the organisation wants to aid integration in the area. It does this by arranging cultural events to inspire dialogue and understanding between different nationalities and religions. They also feed the homeless three times a week.

The church is available to hire for private functions, and can be used for other things besides music, such as lectures and conferences – the acoustics are best for music, though.

Blågårds Church was designed by Andreas Clemmensen and was built between 1925 and 1926. It has a vaulted wooden roof and stained-glass windows made in 1992 by Mogens Jørgensen, who has decorated approximately 25 churches in Denmark and Sweden.

Address Blågårds Plads 6A, 2200 Copenhagen N, www.koncertkirken.dk | Getting there Bus 1A to Prins Jørgens Gade; bus 1A, 5C, 350S to Elmegade | Tip Enjoy Blågårds Square in the middle of the old working-class neighbourhood in Nørrebro, featuring Kai Nielsen's 22 sculptures of workers and children. You could also visit Blågårds Apotek (the Pharmacy), which has been a café, bar and venue since the 1970s.

25__The Coral Bath
Dive in

It could just as well be an outdoor swimming pool, but if you look closely there's something strange about the water … is that seaweed? Hang on, did a little school of fish just swim by? Quite possibly, because the Coral Bath isn't a swimming pool, but one of the Copenhagen Harbour Baths, where you swim in the water from the harbour.

The Coral Bath is made up of pontoons forming a lagoon, which consists of three pools: a paddling pool for the youngest, a kid's pool and a larger pool for swimming. This latter one is very deep, so can only be recommended for experienced swimmers!

The bath gets its popular name from its shape, which is inspired by a coral reef. Its official name, however, is Harbour Bath Sluseholmen, and it was opened as the third harbour bath in Copenhagen in December 2011, when winter bathers were longing to dive in. The other two are found by Islands Brygge and the Fisketorvet shopping centre.

Denmark is a nation of keen bathers, and Copenhageners in particular are crazy for the water, so the three baths are very popular. Even wind and cooler temperatures are no deterrent, and there are people here all year round. Indeed, the bath has its own club of winter bathers, and one pool is equipped with rotating icebreakers throughout the coldest months. On a sunny summer's day, it's almost impossible to find a spot among the hundreds of people who've come to dip their toes, heads or whole bodies in the cool water.

Feel free to join them. The water is as clean as the Øresund, and is checked daily by environmental control, and there are always lifeguards on duty in the summer.

If you prefer chlorine water to the salt variety, you can visit one of Copenhagen's two outdoor swimming pools. One is by Bellahøj in Brønshøj, the other is the Bavnehøj Friluftsbad on Enghavevej, only 2.5 kilometres from the Coral Bath.

Address Ben Websters Vej 69, 2450 Copenhagen SV | Getting there Bus 7A, 18 to Sluseholmen; Harbour Bus 991, 992 to Teglholmen | Hours June–Sept 11am–7pm (out of season it's open to winter bathers at their own risk) | Tip Right next to the Coral Bath is Valby Yacht Club, a nice place to stroll around and look at the boats. And you can enjoy the water from 'above', if you don't feel like going in.

26 __ The Dance Chapel
Dance like no one is watching

Two seven- or eight-year-old boys circle one another in the Brazil-ian martial art capoeira under the instruction of a contra-mestre. The other boys stand around and wait their turn, while a couple of parents watch the proceedings. This is an open house at the Dance Chapel (Dansekapellet), a large rehearsal and performance space for a num-ber of dance companies and other groups dedicated to exercise such as yoga, qigong and of course capoeira, which in this instance takes place in the biggest room, the Domed Hall. This was once used for funerals, but that was long before any of these young martial artists were born.

Some of their parents may have attended funerals here, however, when the studio was the main chapel in the Bispebjerg Cremato-rium. Back then, rows of benches formed a kind of amphitheatre with the coffin in the middle of the room. After the funeral rites, the coffin would be lowered into the floor to the cremation cham-ber, and as friends and family attended a wake at the nearby café, smoke would rise from the tall chimney on the crematorium. The chimney remains, but everything else has long since been removed, and the hall has been made into a dance studio with changing rooms and showers.

You're free to walk around the various studios, and you can have a peek in the changing rooms which have been installed in the for-mer columbarium where the urns were once stored in niches in the walls. These niches have now become lockers for storing the dancers' clothing, and the room is large and bright with columns resembling an ancient temple.

The well-known architect behind the crematorium, Holger Jacobsen (1876–1960), developed a style based on ancient architecture mixed with a little art nouveau. The columns have really come into their own, after previously being hidden in the dark and narrow passages of the columbarium, which is hard to picture now.

Address Bispebjerg Torv 1, 2400 Copenhagen NV, www.dansekapellet.dk | Getting there Bus 4A, 6A to Bispebjerg Torv | Hours Mon–Fri 9am–4pm | Tip Bispebjerg Cemetery still has a columbarium behind the Dance Chapel, and in the cemetery there are Russian, Catholic and Muslim graves, as well as the graves of those who died during the Second World War.

27 — Danish Jewish Museum

The story of the Danish Jews staged by Libeskind

The museum is quite small, but it's somewhat confusing nonetheless. The way through the museum rises and falls, twists and turns and the walls lean in on you in places. It feels like a cave or a wasteland; you can't tell where you're going.

The design of the museum is meant to symbolise the Jews' immigration to and life in Denmark throughout the past 400 years, but also their escape to Sweden in 1943 during the Second World War. The museum was designed by world-renowned architect Daniel Libeskind, who also designed the Jewish museum in Berlin and countless other buildings. He calls the Danish museum Mitzvah, a Hebrew word meaning 'involvement' or 'good deed', as a reference to the Danes who banded together and saved their Jewish countrymen by smuggling them to Sweden in sailing boats during the Nazi occupation of Denmark.

The story is widely known and has become somewhat idealised throughout the years. While it's certainly true that many Danes worked together to aid the Danish Jews in their escape, the story is slightly more nuanced than that. For instance, many were paid for their assistance and most Jews had been warned that an internment was imminent.

The Danish Jewish Museum is worth visiting for its architecture alone, but the permanent exhibition is also thought provoking. Jewish people arrived in Denmark at different times and were assimilated into society quickly and efficiently. In 1814, Jews were granted civil rights but were also forced to submit to Danish law on matters such as schooling and inheritance. When new groups of Jews (especially from Eastern Europe) arrived in the 20th century, however, they had trouble fitting into the Jewish community in Denmark. The museum conveys this diverse history in an engaging manner. It also often hosts special or temporary exhibitions, so check out the website and see what's on.

Address Galejhuset, Proviantpassagen 6, 1218 Copenhagen K, www.jewmus.dk | Getting there Bus 26 to Det Kongelige Bibliotek; bus 2A, 23, 31, 37 to Stormbroen/National-museet; bus 2A, 23, 32, 37 or Metro M3 to Gammel Strand | Hours 1 June–31 Aug, Tue–Sun 10am–5pm; 1 Sept–31 May, Tue–Fri 1–4pm, Sat & Sun noon–5pm | Tip The museum is situated in the garden of the Royal Library (Bibliotekshaven). Calm and withdrawn from the bustle of inner-city life, it's a favourite of many Copenhageners.

28 __ The Danish Music Museum

A house filled with music

Music and singing feature heavily in the former Radio House on Rosenørns Allé. The Royal Danish Academy of Music is housed here, and there are frequent rehearsals and auditions, which can be heard in the halls and stairways. There are also regular performances in the Academy's concert hall. You can play too, since the Danish Music Museum (Musikmuseet) is on the third floor of the building, where you can try your hand at pianos, harps, drums and electric guitars. The instruments are replaced from time to time, so you never know what will be there on your next visit.

The 'Sound Room' is specially soundproofed, allowing you to play the different instruments without disturbing others, but you can also just walk around and admire the museum's large collection of different instruments while listening to the music they make when played well. It's easy to lose track of time while marvelling at rare Renaissance instruments or the Wurlitzer organ, which was once used in cinemas.

The museum has one of Europe's best collections of historical instruments from all over the world. It was founded in 1898 by Angul Hammerich (1848–1931), who was an expert in Bronze Age lurs, among other things. The museum was originally part of the Museum of Decorative Arts (see ch. 47), but became a separate institution in the 1960s, and was merged with another large collection of instruments belonging to the manufacturer Carl Claudius (1855–1931) in 1977. In 2009, it became part of the National Museum and in 2014, it moved into newly renovated rooms in the former Radio House.

The museum can be hard to find, but if you do get lost, at least you can enjoy the building, which is a masterpiece of Danish architecture.

Address Rosenørns Allé 22, 1972 Frederiksberg C, www.en.natmus.dk/museums/ the-danish-music-museum | **Getting there** Bus 2A, 71, 250S or Metro M 1, M 2 to Forum | **Hours** Sat & Sun 10am–4pm (the Academy is closed at weekends and in July) | **Tip** If you turn right at the reception desk, go down the stairs to the foyer of the concert hall, continue on to a stairway and go to the third floor, you'll find the cafeteria and courtyard, which have barely been changed since the Radio House was built in 1945.

29__Danish National Art Library

Atmospheric and historic reference library

In May 2000, the great hall in the University of Copenhagen's Frederiksberg Campus (see ch. 109) was irrevocably damaged in a gas explosion. When it reopened two years later, it had been restored according to the original drawings and the original painter's proposed colours and decorations.

All of these old drawings were found in the archives of the Danish National Art Library (Danmarks Kunstbibliotek), which contains 300,000 technical drawings from the past 400 years, in addition to the largest collection of art history literature in the Nordic countries.

The library opened in 1754 as a reference library for the newly established Royal Academy of Fine Arts in the palace of Charlottenborg. The library collection evolved over the centuries, and in 2004 it became the Danish National Art Library. At the same time, a significant part of its archives were moved into storage, and during the move a veritable treasure was found: 65 forgotten drawings by designer Poul Henningsen, or PH. The great Danish designer is known internationally for, among other things, his PH Artichoke Lamp, and after the rediscovery of the drawings, a furniture company quickly put into production the long-forgotten furniture designs.

Since the 1880s, the library has been situated in a wing of the art gallery Kunsthal Charlottenborg. Most visitors to the exhibitions at Charlottenborg probably don't even notice the rather unassuming entrance. While the library was a part of the Royal Academy of Fine Arts, it was slightly run-down, but was given an overhaul when it became a separate institution in 1996. Not only was the library refurbished, but the collections were digitised, meaning that you can search them from home, just as you can search the art history archives and various bibliographies and lexica. Since research is thirsty work, there's also a café in Kunsthal Charlottenborg which hosts small exhibitions.

Address Nyhavn 2, 1007 Copenhagen K, www.kunstbib.dk | **Getting there** Bus 23 or Metro M1, M2, M3 to Kongens Nytorv | **Hours** Mon–Thu 11am–5.30pm, Fri 11am–4pm. During summer Mon–Fri 11am–4pm | **Tip** Charlottenborg itself is a palace from the 1670s and houses the Royal Danish Academy of Fine Arts' administration and banquet hall, which is open from time to time.

30__ The Danish National Bank

If you're in the mood for newly minted money

If you need crisp banknotes or newly minted coins (perhaps for a birthday present) you can withdraw them from the cashier at the National Bank (Nationalbanken), where you can also exchange money that's looking slightly worse for wear. In order to get there, you'll have to go through the inconspicuous main entrance, which leads 'visitors down a slightly downwards-sloping floor through the curved corridor into the high-ceilinged vestibule', in the words of the architect.

The word vestibule is somewhat of an understatement. It has a 20-metre-high ceiling, and the room looks more like a cathedral with its tall, narrow windows. The walls are covered with Norwegian marble and the only furniture is six of Arne Jacobsen's (1902–1971) Swan chairs. He designed the whole building, as well as the Vola tap, the Lilly chair and the appropriately named Banker's Clock.

In order to make way for the building, an entire residential block was demolished in the 1960s and 1970s, along with the old National Bank from 1870. Jacobsen didn't see this as a problem. He was, however, worried that his building would have a negative effect on the neighbouring buildings – Holmen's Church and Børsen (the former Stock Exchange). He was placated by the artistic advisors to the state, the Academy Council, who told him that neither of the buildings' exteriors were authentic enough to warrant such worry.

Incidentally, Arne Jacobsen practically drove his employees and the developer mad with his insistence on using only the finest materials. For instance the wooden panelling in the office areas – European pear wood for the walls and African Douisse wood for the floors – had to be discarded if there was the smallest fault in the timber. Those areas are, however, not open to the public, and neither are the rooftop gardens, which cover the whole roof of the building. Here, Jacobsen was forced to submit to the mandatory requirement that no plants be tall enough for someone to hide in them – as a matter of security.

Address Havnegade 5, 1093 Copenhagen K, www.nationalbanken.dk | Getting there Bus 23, 26 to Holmens Kirke; bus 2A, 31, 37 to Børsen | Hours Vestibule: Mon–Fri 9am–4pm; cashier: Mon–Fri 10am–1pm | Tip At Holmens Kanal 2 is the headquarters of Danske Bank, which contains the most impressive banking interior from times past. There is also a cash machine that dispenses Euros.

31 The David Collection
A world-class collection of Islamic art

The Danish prime minister's official residence is Marienborg, situated just north of Copenhagen, which was bequeathed to the Danish state by the heirless attorney and businessman Christian Ludvig David (1878–1960).

Few Danes today would associate C. L. David with Marienborg, though many will associate him with the David Collection, because in addition to being a businessman, David was also something of a collector. His collection contains European ceramics and furniture from the 18th century, Danish silverware and some paintings, including 11 paintings by prominent Danish artist Vilhelm Hammershøi, renowned for his muted, poetic interiors. The main part of the David Collection, however, is Islamic art, especially Persian ceramics. This part of the collection is one of the 10 most significant in the Western world.

David's collection was originally stored on the top floor of the building in Kronprinssessegade which he purchased in 1918. It grew and grew, and in 1945 David decided that the building should be an independent foundation with private funds – lots of them – to expand the collection. There was a rapid expansion after his death, and the whole house (which incidentally is preserved in its original state with early 19th-century interiors) became a museum. Throughout the 1960s and 1970s, the collection came to include English 18th-century furniture, and Islamic art spanning the period from the 8th to the 19th centuries from practically the whole of the Islamic world.

Before it was rebuilt between 2005 and 2009, the museum was rather old-fashioned and not very well known, but the refurbishment has meant that visitors can now see the many treasures within impressive modern settings. The museum is so popular, in fact, that it informs visitors that there are likely to be many school groups, especially in the mornings.

Address Kronprinsessegade 30, 1306 Copenhagen K, www.davidmus.dk | **Hours** Sun – Tue 10am – 5pm, Wed 10am – 9pm | **Tip** The museum is situated across from the 17th-century Rosenborg Castle and its gardens (Kongens Have). The gardens now form a public park with both historical and modern elements and a number of activities throughout the year, including concerts and theatre performances.

32 ___ The Deer in Ørestad

Denmark's longest piece of street art

It's like a fairy tale: the deer venturing into the unknown. At first it encounters no obstacles, then it reaches the forest and moves past the first tree trunks. The trees soon get closer, and the deer is well on its way, where no one knows what to expect. It's swallowed up by the darkness among the trees, and we can no longer follow it. Where is it? What happened? Will we see it again?

We will, mercifully, as it appears a few metres further along, popping up between the trees. It has overcome the darkness and is now heading out into the sun, into the light – towards us. Oh good, it all ended well!

In/between is the name of this painting, which at 271 metres is the longest piece of street art in Denmark. It has adorned the fence between Bella Center and Ørestad Boulevard since the spring of 2013 and was created by the Argentinian street artist Hyuro.

The decoration of the fence was chosen in a competition that was organised by the City of Copenhagen and Rebel Agency. Of the 140 artists from around the world who submitted entries, Hyuro's idea of a deer in perpetual motion won.

Located right at the beginning of Ørestad Boulevard, the deer also helps to welcome you to Ørestad, one of Copenhagen's newest neighbourhoods. As a spectator, you can stand still and watch the deer in one place, but you're not really in touch with the deer and its way in and out of the forest until you've followed it – by bike, car, running or walking. This makes you a part of the 271-metre-long adventure.

Continuing on your way through Ørestad City, just after the motorway bridge you come upon the new concert and sports hall of Copenhagen, the Royal Arena. It was designed by 3XN Architects and opened in 2017, and this is another story that ended well: for many years, Copenhagen has been missing a large sports arena capable of attracting both national and international events.

Address Ørestad Boulevard, 2300 Copenhagen S | Getting there Bus 18, 34, 77 or Metro M1 to Bella Center | Tip At vimeo.com/57490706 you can see a 43-second animation of the deer's path through the woods.

33 DieselHouse

(Formerly) the world's largest diesel engine

There is an overpowering smell of petroleum at the DieselHouse. But that can hardly come as a surprise in a museum built up around an enormous double-acting two-stroke diesel engine from 1932. It was once the largest diesel engine in the world, built for the H. C. Ørsted Power Station and attached to a 15-MW generator which provided electricity to the people of Copenhagen. The engine was operational until the 1970s, and was used until 2004 as a backup engine in case of power outages. Since then it has been the main attraction at the DieselHouse.

When standing in front of the engine, it's not hard to imagine that it really was once the largest in the world. It's switched on every first and third Sunday of each month at 11am, and if you're the least bit interested in the sputter and noise of machinery, you should go and see this behemoth in action.

The museum has more to offer than just this engine, though. It spans four floors and relates the story of the diesel engine and its significance, and the story of B&W – once the largest shipyard and producer of diesel engines in Denmark. At its peak, it was the largest employer in Denmark with thousands of workers, and when politicians and labour unions discussed industrial relations, they would often ask: 'What's the verdict from B&W?'

While the B&W exhibition may be somewhat self-aggrandising at times (the museum is owned by MAN Diesel & Turbo, who bought up B&W in 1979), it is nonetheless an important and interesting part of the history of Danish industry and labour. Furthermore, the exhibition contains numerous models of oil tankers and machines from the factory floor, so a good time is to be had by walking around and turning them all on to see how they work.

DieselHouse is located in Sydhavnen, once a major industrial area, although these days the only functioning trace of its industrial past is the H. C. Ørsted Power Station.

Address Elværksvej 50, 2450 Copenhagen SV (entrance from Vasbygade for pedestrians and bicyclists), www.dieselhouse.dk | Getting there Bus 7A to H. C. Ørstedsværket; bus 10 or S-train A, B, Bx, C, E, I I to Dybbølsbro | Hours Tue–Fri 10am–4pm, first and third Sunday of each month 10am–1.30pm | Tip A walk will take you to Støbegodsvej 1, where you'll find Supermarco, which sells Italian specialities. Enjoy a freshly brewed espresso, while the lady in the delicatessen slices mortadella or pecorino for you.

34 The Elephant House

Tying the Zoo and Frederiksberg Gardens together

In November 2013, there was a hubbub in Copenhagen Zoo's new elephant enclosure. Males and females are usually kept separate, but the male elephant Cheing-Mai, who came to the zoo in 1962, was introduced to the females in their part of the enclosure. One of the females instantly ran away into the deep pool, while the others circled Cheing-Mai, trumpeting and banging their trunks on the ground. The purpose of this visit was to impregnate the female Surin. This was, incidentally, a success.

Copenhagen Zoo goes to great lengths to get their elephants to mate, and that means making sure the elephants are healthy. For many years they lived under fairly poor conditions in an enclosure built in 1914, which was both small and old-fashioned. However, in 2008 they could finally move into a new, bigger enclosure. In addition to ensuring the well-being of these large residents, the enclosure was also meant to tie the zoo and Frederiksberg Gardens together. The enclosure was therefore built in such a way that patrons of the zoo can see the elephants with the gardens in the background, and visitors to the gardens can see the elephants. The landscaped paddock is built to resemble a dry riverbed near a deep, sinuous pool – so deep that you occasionally only see the tip of a trunk sticking out of it.

The construction of the enclosure had its technological challenges. A fully-grown Asian elephant like Cheing-Mai weighs five and a half tonnes, and it was necessary to put a lift in at the bottom of the pool to ensure that, should he be unable to get out of there by himself, there will be no need to call in cranes. The weight and strength of the elephants also meant that strong walls were needed for the enclosure, but since the elephants were to be visible from Frederiksberg Gardens, this was not an easy task. Calculations from ship collisions were used to construct durable fences and posts, made to be as discreet as possible, thus allowing for a free elephant sighting on your garden walk.

Address Copenhagen Zoo: Roskildevej 32, 2000 Frederiksberg; Frederiksberg Gardens: entrances on Roskildevej, Søndre Fasanvej, Porcelænshaven, Smallegade and Frederiksberg Runddel, www.zoo.dk | Getting there Bus 7A, 72 to Zoologisk Have (where you can also enter Frederiksberg Gardens) | Hours The Zoo opens at 10am on weekdays, 9am at weekends, closing times change throughout the year, but no earlier than 4pm. See website for more details. Frederiksberg Gardens are open from 6am to 5pm or 11pm depending on the time of year. | Tip Porcelænshaven is on the premises of the former Royal Copenhagen factory, which was a town within the town. The area is located a short walk through the gardens from the elephant enclosure – aim for the old chimney.

35＿Enghave Park

From dance parties to flooding control

Entering Enghave Park after the autumn of 2019, you won't just be in a park, but in one of the most ambitious food control projects in Europe. The park has been chosen to take on rainwater from large parts of Vesterbro, and should there be a cloudburst, the bandstand will be the only dry place in sight.

The renovation project is an extensive one, but after it Vesterbro's public park will still look largely as when it was established in the late 1920s – a symmetrical layout with a bandstand at one end and a basin with fountains at the other. Apart from these, the park contains a playing field for ball games and two gardens, one for roses and one for perennial plants. Both are excellent places to sit and enjoy the trickling fountains or the laughter of children playing in the water.

The architect responsible for the bandstand was unknown until recently, when it was discovered that he was none other than the young Arne Jacobsen (1902–1971), now recognised as one of Denmark's most prominent architects and designers. This discovery significantly increased interest in the bandstand from foundations and conservation authorities.

The bandstand will bring back many memories for older Copenhageners, as it was the site of summer dance parties from 1958 to 1964, where one could jitterbug and twist to the sounds of the new rock'n'roll bands. These nights are long gone, however, and with the establishment of green courtyards in the residential areas during the 1990s, the park came to be used less and less. The people involved in the new Enghave Park hope that this development will be turned around with the renovations, which will maintain some of the old elements, while introducing more 'sensual stimulation' and allowing for more movement such as street hockey and cricket. And instead of summer dance parties, the ground in front of the bandstand will hopefully see some winter activity with the opening of a brand-new skating rink.

Address Enghavevej, 1674 Copenhagen V, www.tredjenatur.dk/portfolio/enghaveparken-her-og-nu | Getting there Bus 1A or Metro M3 Enghave Plads | Tip There are numerous cafés and bars on Enghavevej (between the concert venue Vega and Matthæusgade), many of them with outdoor seating and good opportunities for having a coffee in the sun.

36__F. Petitgas Eftf.

Gentlemen's hats since 1857

'Eftf.' is an abbreviation of the word *efterfølgere* meaning 'successor', which was a common way of carrying on (or perhaps exploiting) your predecessor's good name. Petitgas' shop has been selling men's hats since 1857, when the French hatter François Petitgas (1825–1913) set up shop in Copenhagen. He lived in the house with his Danish wife and daughter, and in the back house he maintained a millinery with several employees. Rumour has it that fairy-tale author H. C. Andersen bought his famous top hats here, and there's a story that both Frederik IX of Denmark and Olav V of Norway once showed up on the same day for a fitting.

When Petitgas died, his widow, Caroline, ran the shop until 1924, when she sold it to his first successor, Anton Rasmussen, whose son and grandson ran the shop until 1981. Until 2013, one successor replaced the next until there was no one left to take over when the owner retired. Bernhard Tommerup, a long-time patron of the shop, couldn't bear the idea of the shop closing, and so he left his job at IBM and bought it. Tommerup has kept much of the original interior: the cupboards are the originals from 1857, while the ceilings, register and latticed window are from 1892, when the shop went from using gas to electricity.

The classic hats from F. Petitgas Eftf. are made from rabbit, hare or beaver, but you can also purchase silk hats, felt hats, straw hats and cowboy hats. Several shops in Copenhagen sold these types of hat until the late 1990s, when only Petitgas' shop remained. Some new shops have opened recently, however.

F. Petitgas Eftf. is one of the few specialist shops left in Købmager-gade, which is thought to be the oldest street in Copenhagen. Un-til the 1960s and 1970s, there were many different shops, especially food shops such as butchers, fishmongers and cheesemongers. The name Købmagergade, in fact, roughly translates to 'Butcher's Street', although this isn't apparent to most Copenhageners.

Address Købmagergade 5, 1150 Copenhagen K, www.petitgas.dk | Getting there
Bus 2A, 23, 32, 37 or Metro M3 to Gammel Strand | Hours Tue–Fri 11am–5.30pm,
Sat 11am–3pm | Tip Franz Jaeger & Me (Gothersgade 31) also sells men's hats, and
C.L. Seifert (Ny Adelgade 8–10) sells hats and graduation caps – a proud Danish
tradition. If you see someone wearing a white cap with a black visor in June or July,
feel free to congratulate them.

37__The Fishing Harbour in Nordhavn

A pocket of tranquillity

It's no small feat to find the Fishing Harbour at the very tip of the Nordhavn peninsula (if you're lucky enough to have a navigational system handy, put in 'Jacob Jensens Bådeværft' to make sure you arrive at the right place), but once you've made it to this 'outpost' of containers, sheds, twine, fishing boats, house boats and dinghies, it's worth the hassle. The view of Østerbro and Hellerup is spectacular, first and foremost, but the harbour itself is a little pocket of calm, where you can take a break on one of the benches, or perhaps have a chat with some of the local boat owners.

Nordhavn is quickly becoming the newest neighbourhood in Copenhagen. The man-made peninsula was filled in in the late 18th century, and it was a working industrial area and free port until the 1970s. Now there are several housing and commercial developments, providing all manner of modern comforts for wealthy Copenhagen families, and on nordhavnen.dk, you can see the vision for the area. The Fishing Harbour is in stark contrast to these developments – a reminder of the history of the harbour. The boat owners still refuse to have water (and sanitation) installed in their sheds. If you ask the locals, this is partly to avoid the rent going up, but also to make sure that the area doesn't become a holiday camp for rich Copenhageners.

The Fishing Harbour used to be further in on Nordhavn, but in 1995–1996, the City moved the boats and sheds to their new position in collaboration with their owners. It was originally a fishing village, but as everywhere else in the country, fishing has diminished due to EU quotas, falling prices and increased bureaucracy, or so the locals say. Today only a few fishermen remain. However, active sailing clubs and small boating businesses have sprung up, so local engagement in the area remains high.

Address Fiskerihavnen (Skudehavnen), Østersøvej, 2150 Nordhavn | Getting there
Bus 27 to Nordsøvej | Tip If you're an early riser, you can begin at the fish market, where
you can walk among salmon, lobsters, oysters and the restaurateurs of Copenhagen, who
go to pick out seafood for their restaurants. Unfortunately, the fishmongers can only sell
to restaurants and businesses and not private individuals.

38 Frederiksberg Flea Market

Find a bargain among a wide selection of items

Behind the large city hall in the municipality of Frederiksberg, with its 70-metre-tall tower, is one of the best flea markets in town. It's also one of the biggest, with 93 stalls (48 large and 45 small) and is open from early April until late October.

The residents of Frederiksberg have their choice of the stalls, which means ordinary people and amateur salesmen make up the bulk of the sellers here. However, there are also professional dealers here, but they're usually easy to spot due to their large selection of items, and prices that are generally higher and more difficult to barter down than elsewhere.

If you're hunting for a real bargain, you should arrive early. The market officially opens at 9am, but the first sellers arrive at 6 or 7am to set up their stalls, mainly to be able to park nearby. Collectors (e.g. of postcards, LPs or photographic equipment) arrive at about the same time, as do the professional dealers, in order to secure bargains which they can in turn resell in shops or online. At about 8 or 9am, they move on to the next market, while locals and other interested parties browse the stalls for the remainder of the day, looking for designer shoes, trinkets for the house or children's clothing. There are usually stalls with tools and various metal things which attract many customers, although they could probably find newer and cheaper things at the local DIY shop. The same goes for things like crockery and cutlery, but here they have some kind of history, and you have a more interesting story of how you came by them. Sometimes you can find nice old ladies who are selling off their possessions, or younger people selling unwanted heirlooms or whole estates, which can make for some interesting purchases.

Around closing time at 3pm, you can usually get discounted items, but you'll rarely find very valuable items, as they're normally sold online. In general, you should only pay what you feel comfortable paying.

Address Smallegade / Frederiksberg Bredegade (behind Frederiksberg City Hall), 2000 Frederiksberg | Getting there Bus 9A, 31 to Frederiksberg Bredegade; bus 9A, 18, 31, 71, 72, 74 to Frederiksberg Rådhus or Metro M1, M2, M3 to Frederiksberg | Hours Apr–Oct, Sat 9am–3pm | Tip There are approximately 10 regular outdoor flea markets in the Copenhagen area, and many more which are only open a few times a year. See copenhagen.com / shopping for more information.

39 Frederiksberg Hill

A view of historic Copenhagen

Few places in Copenhagen allow you to behold the entire historic town centre with its towers and rooftops. Kløvermarken on Amager (see ch. 11) is one of them, the hill in Bellahøj is another, and then there's Frederiksberg Hill (Frederiksberg Bakke). According to an old tradition, if you go up here on an early Whitsun morning, you can even see the sun 'dance' over the rooftops. This concept is probably derived from the Catholic parts of Europe, where it was said that the sun would dance with joy on Easter Sunday in celebration of the resurrection. In Denmark, this tradition has been moved to Whitsun (40 days after Easter), when there is a better chance of sunshine, and perhaps to coincide with an older celebration of the coming of spring. This event was celebrated (among other places) on Solbjerget (the Sun Mountain), the original name of the hill. Today it's called Frederiksberg Hill on the side that overlooks Frederiksberg Palace and Gardens, while the opposite side is called Valby Hill (Valby Bakke).

Solbjerget must have been especially noticeable in the Copenhagen of the past, as it makes a steep climb in an otherwise flat landscape. Other hills in the outskirts of Copenhagen are higher, but have a more gradual climb.

The high hill is also the main reason why Frederiksberg Palace was built on this spot. It was built by the crown prince (who later became King Frederik IV), who was greatly inspired by the princely mountainside palaces he had seen on his travels in Italy. He was also enamoured with French formal gardens, so when he ascended the throne in 1699, he initiated the construction of Frederiksberg Palace in the style of an Italian palace with a French baroque garden. In the late 18th century, the gardens were open to the public on special occasions, and were permanently opened in the mid-19th century. At that point, the garden had been redesigned as an English landscape garden with a temple, waterfall and grotto, and today the park is one of the most popular in the city.

Address Frederiksberg Palace, Roskildevej 28A, 2000 Frederiksberg | Getting there
Bus 7A, 72 to Zoologisk Have | Tip The palace now houses the Royal Danish Military
Academy. There are public tours at weekends, in English on the last Saturday of the month
(except for July and December), at 11am and 1pm. You can try to order group tours in
foreign languages at frederiksbergslot.dk. The palace chapel is a working parish church
and is open in connection with masses and other church ceremonies.

40_ The Frederikshøj Allotments

Build your own dream house

The heart of any DIY enthusiast is sure to race a little when walking around the Frederikshøj Allotments. Here you can build your very own dream house and experiment with materials and decoration.

The community was founded in 1923 and was originally meant to house the working-class citizens of Copenhagen, as long as they were willing to build their own houses. As money was often tight, refuse such as wooden boxes or other packaging from the local factories would be used as building materials for simple wooden houses. There was no heating, electricity or running water, and the buildings were not regulated – you could build whatever you wanted in the space available.

These days there's central heating and drainage, and all the houses have both running water and electricity. The community has rules regarding the height and size of the houses, and the City has put out a local development plan. Yet this hasn't stifled people's creativity, and the houses still look very different from one another – not out of necessity, but desire and imagination. There are round or crooked windows, taken from construction waste around town, set in architect-drawn, sustainable houses, which stand side by side with brick-walled buildings, where shapes and colours have no limits. There are even a few old shacks left which have been here almost as long as the community itself.

There are 193 houses with room for approximately 500 residents. Community spirit is high and there are many common activities, such as the 'maternity club', which for over 30 years has been providing new parents with home-cooked meals for the first weeks after their baby arrives.

Some residents rent their houses out through Airbnb, so if you want you can stay there for a night or two.

Address H/F Frederikshøj, 2450 Copenhagen SV | **Getting there** Bus 7A, 9A, 18, 23 to Mozarts Plads; bus 9A to Stubmøllevej or Valbyparken | **Tip** From Frederikshøj you can walk straight across to the largest park in Copenhagen: the Valby Park. If you're cycling, you can go out to the Kystager Park, and – if you and the weather are up to it – on along the cycle paths to Hvidovre Havn, across Avedøre Holme, on to Brøndby Strand and perhaps all the way down to Arken Museum of Modern Art in Ishøj, roughly a 14-kilometre trip.

41 The Gaol in Slutterigade
A classicist masterpiece

At dusk, a horse-drawn Black Maria turns onto the cobblestones of Slutterigade. The gas lamps have just been lit, and the wagon casts long shadows on the courthouse walls as the driver stops in front of the gaol. The delinquent is escorted out and cowers at the sight of the imposing door before him. *For the security of the public* is chiselled above the door, and then it hits him – he will spend the next year on bread and water. For the first time he repents and realises what he has done.

Perhaps this is how architect C. F. Hansen (1756–1845) imagined prisoners would react when they were taken to the gaol in Slutterigade. The building's overpowering and strongly defined architecture signals that all hope is lost. There is no unnecessary ornamentation, only sharp, harsh lines signifying the treatment awaiting lawbreakers. Woe unto him that breaks the law of the land and is put in jail!

The large arches at each end make the short street feel claustrophobic. It closes in on itself, as if the gaol begins at the very entrance, before you've even reached the cells.

The gaol was built in 1805–1815, and is a prime example of architecture parlante – speaking architecture – explaining its own purpose.

C. F. Hansen was commissioned to build a new courthouse after the Copenhagen Fire of 1795 claimed – among other things – the old courthouse and city hall. He was also responsible for the gaol, which was attached to the courthouse by the two arches containing secret passages. The gaol is widely regarded as the masterpiece of his classicist works.

Only the façades towards Slutterigade, Hestemøllerstræde and the courtyard still remain as they were designed by Hansen; everything else disappeared in the refurbishments during the late 19th and mid-20th centuries. The city hall was moved in 1905, but the courthouse and gaol are still in use today.

Address Københavns Arrest (Copenhagen Gaol), Slutterigade 1, 1461 Copenhagen K | Getting there Bus 2A, 23, 31, 37 to Stormbroen / Nationalmuseet; bus 2A, 5C, 250S, 10, 23, 33 or Metro M 3 to Rådhuspladsen | Tip You can find many other examples of C. F. Hansen's work within walking distance of Slutterigade: Vor Frue Kirke (The Church of Our Lady) on Frue Plads; Metropolitanskolen (which now houses part of the University of Copenhagen) in Fiolstræde; Trøstens Bolig (The House of Comfort – a dwelling for paupers) in Vestergade as well as the Chapel at Christiansborg Palace.

42__The Garden Society Gardens
Perfect for a wedding

Through the gate on the left-hand side of the main entrance to Frederiksberg Gardens (Frederiksberg Have), you can enter the Garden Society Gardens. It's the size of two football pitches (approximately 14,000 square metres), and was established in the 1880s according to the designs of the most famous landscape architect of the time, H. A. Flindt (1822–1901). The purpose was to exhibit different kinds of private gardens, and there is a Japanese garden and an azalea garden to name but a few of around 20 different kinds. Behind the garden itself, there are 83 allotments that are rented out to the members of the Garden Society.

The Garden Society has approximately 45,000 members nationwide and has its headquarters in Søborg, to the northwest of Copenhagen. It traces its roots back to 1830, when the Danish Garden Society was founded, inspired by similar societies in England. In 1880, it could add 'Royal' to its name as an appreciation of its work, and to distinguish it from two other societies elsewhere in Denmark. When the three merged, they settled on the name The Garden Society.

The gardens are open to the public all day, and there's more to see than just plants. There are often art exhibitions and concerts in Brøndsalen (The Well Hall), and it's also used for wedding receptions, so if you get married at Frederiksberg City Hall, you can stroll through the gardens on your way to the reception. The room got its name in the late 19th century, when the wealthy members would meet there to drink spring water.

The restaurant Mielcke & Hurtigkarl often hosts large events and utilises the plants from the gardens in their 'New Nordic' cuisine. The restaurant is located in one of the wings of a little 17th-century palace, the main wing of which burned down in 1753 and the main entrance to the Frederiksberg Gardens was put in its place.

Address Frederiksberg Runddel 1, 2000 Frederiksberg, www.haveselskabet.dk | **Getting there** Bus 18, 26, 71, 72 to Frederiksberg Runddel; Metro M 3 to Frederiksberg Allé | **Tip** You can get married in the park (or everywhere else) if you get an official or a member of the City Council to marry you.

43　The Garderhøj Fort
Join the defence of Copenhagen!

The children run around shouting joyfully at each other, shooting cannonballs at Lyngby Lake or climbing around the gym. This may not sound like acceptable museum behaviour, but the Garderhøj Fort is a museum nevertheless.

The old fortification – built between 1885 and 1892 – is now used as an experience centre and hands-on museum for children and their parents. It can also be booked for children's birthday parties, should they want to try something other than Tivoli or McDonald's. There are many things to experience at the fort; apart from using the gymnasium or the child-sized cannon, you can try your hand at operating the telegraph, cooking and eating in the mess, writing with an old-fashioned fountain pen and taking a (well-deserved) nap in the bunks.

It's also well worth the walk up the tallest tower to see the two iron cannons, where you'll get a sense of just how much manpower it took to operate the cannons, and you're allowed to touch both cannonballs and grenades.

The Garderhøj Fort was built as the largest land-based part of the fortifications of Copenhagen, and was meant to keep enemies out. Rather unusually, the funds for building the fort in the 1880s were raised through a private association, as the local residents felt that the government was taking too long to decide where to build them. Mostly from private contributions, but also through lotteries, bazaars and performances, they raised 1.5 million DKK, the equivalent of 106 million DKK today. Having built the fort, they leased it to the War Ministry. Only 28 years after it was built, however, all the fortifications were closed down, since they were no match for modern warfare. The Garderhøj Fort was then used as an ammunitions store and a training ground for both the army and the police. In 1992 it was given back to the Danish people and, after a thorough restoration, it was opened to the public in 2013.

Address Garderhøjfort 4, 2820 Gentofte, www.garderhojfort.dk | Getting there S-train A, E to Jægersborg; bus 179 to Jægersborg, Ibstrupvej | Hours Sat, Sun & bank holidays 10.30am–4pm, Mon–Tue by appointment only | Tip If you just can't get enough of Copenhagen's old fortifications, you can visit Western Fortification Activity Centre at the Ejby Bunker; go to the beach by Charlottenlund Fort, or walk along the Western Fortifications, now a 15-kilometre-long park running from Avedøre to Utterslev Mose, which is perfect for a picnic.

44 Garnisons Cemetery and Holmens Cemetery

The famous and the unknown from the Schleswig Wars

The Schleswig Wars of 1848–1850 and 1864 left deep wounds in Denmark and still remain an inexhaustible source of interest today. While they were fought far from Copenhagen, on and around the German border, there are many traces of the wars to be found in the city, especially in the Garnisons and Holmens cemeteries, where there are numerous graves and memorials to those who gave their lives.

If you begin your journey at Garnisons Cemetery (at the end closest to Østerport Station), you'll find an obelisk erected as a memorial for both wars. Across from this is a mass grave for 226 soldiers who died in the second war of 1864 – they were originally buried separately, but their graves were removed in the 1880s.

At the opposite end of the cemetery, you'll find Major General Rye, who led an assault that broke the siege of Fredericia in 1849. Close by are a number of graves belonging to those who fell at the Battle of Dybbøl 1864, a famous battle which is commemorated each year in Southern Jutland. Next to them is General de Meza, who was responsible for the evacuation of Danevirke, an ancient fortification central to the Danish identity. At the time, many Danes were outraged that de Meza should abandon Danevirke, which remains a part of Germany as a result of the war.

If you cross the street into Holmens Cemetery, you'll find the only sailor to have died at Dybbøl: William Balduin Jespersen, who served aboard the ironclad *Rolf Krake*. At the end of the lane lies Christian Krieger, who tried to rescue his wounded men from a burning ship before it exploded in Eckernförde Bay in 1849.

The politician Orla Lehmann, who coined the phrase 'Denmark to the Eider' (i.e. that the Eider River should form the border between Denmark and Germany – meaning that the Duchy of Schleswig should be part of Denmark), is also buried here.

Address Garnisons Kirkegård, 2100 Copenhagen Ø; Holmens Kirkegård, 2100 Copenhagen Ø | Getting there Bus 23, 27; Metro M 3 or S-train A, B, Bx, C, E, H to Østerport | Tip If you walk from Østerport Station towards Kastellet, you'll find a little path that leads through the first rampart up towards the moat surrounding Kastellet. Here you'll find a memorial to the many volunteers who came from Norway and Sweden to fight with the Danish army during the Schleswig Wars.

45 The Genetically Modified Paradise

Being human

Most of us are familiar with Edvard Eriksen's classic sculpture *The Little Mermaid*, inspired by Hans Christian Andersen's fairy tale. Artist Bjørn Nørgaard, however, has a somewhat different interpretation of the story: the mermaid is genetically modified, because she uses magic to change her body in order to get her prince. It ends badly – only in Disney's version do they live happily ever after.

According to Nørgaard, if you overstep your boundaries, you face the consequences. This is also evident in his own mermaid, which is situated near Eriksen's classic sculpture, and which forms part of the sculpture group the Genetically Modified Paradise. The figures twist and turn, and this effect is amplified when reflected in the water. It's visually striking, but Nørgaard's intention is not to impress, but rather make us reflect on what it means to be human in modern society.

The central figure is a sinking triumphal arch, with a split, swirling woman's body on top: the Madonna. Nørgaard wants his audience to consider how technological developments – for better or worse – change our perception of what the human body is and what it can do. He explains in an interview on his website that he explores, 'what kind of an entity the human being actually is, what it looks like – and what it will look like in 100 or 200 years. And the "Genetically Altered Female Figure, or Madonna" on top of the Triumphal Arch is a completely wildly growing manifestation of what might conceivably happen if we just let the forces loose without anybody bothering to consider what the consequences might be.'

The genetically modified mermaid sits alone on a stone in the harbour basin, while the others are gathered in a pool by Dahlerup's Warehouse. The sculptures were created for the Danish pavilion at the World's Fair in Hannover in 2000 and were moved to their current location in 2006.

Address Dahlerups Pakhus, Langelinie Allé, 2100 Copenhagen Ø | Getting there Bus 27 to Langeliniekaj | Tip Take a walk through the tiny Langelinie Park. Here you'll find a memorial for the warship *Dannebrog*, which was blown up in 1710 during a battle against Sweden in the Great Northern War. The cannon barrels at the foot of the memorial are from the ship itself.

46__Gentofte Fire Museum

Lighting fires in the hearts of young and old

This is the place for anyone who's ever dreamed of being a fireman – regardless of how old you are. Beautiful old fire engines from as far back as the 1910s fill the sheds at Gentofte's old fire station, which is now a museum.

In addition, you can see the varying trends in uniforms, fire hydrants, smoke detectors and much more. You're allowed to touch most things at the museum, meaning that you can play at being a fireman in a real fire engine (although you have to sit in the passenger seats in the back), or you can let the children try a fire bicycle or sound the alarms.

The fire station was built in 1901 but was decommissioned in 1939. The museum has been housed here in the beautiful old building – almost worth a visit in its own right – since 1987. It is run by dedicated volunteers who are happy to show you around and answer any questions you might have. Their enthusiasm for the place is evident and somewhat contagious.

It's hard not to be impressed when you see fire engines like the one from 1939, which is equipped with a ladder that weighs 8 tonnes and can reach the top of the Hellerup Church tower, which stands 36 metres tall. Don't believe us? They have the pictures to prove it! They also have a great deal of material that showcases the development of fire brigade work from the mid-19th century until today. Looking at the old suits of protective clothing, the leather fire buckets and hoses and the manually controlled pumps, you cannot help but marvel at the ingenuity, bravery and hard work that the firemen of the past put into keeping their cities safe.

If your visit to the museum hasn't satisfied your interest in historical firefighting, the people responsible for this museum have also put up exhibitions in two other fire stations, in Jægersborg (on Ermelundsvej 96X) and at Charlottenlund Palace (on Jægersborg Allé 2a). Both feature 19th-century firefighting equipment.

Address Hellerupvej 5B, 2900 Hellerup, www.gentoftebrandmuseum.dk | **Getting there** S-train A, C, E to Hellerup; bus 1A, 21, 23, 164, 171, 172, 179 to Strandvejen | **Hours** Wed 10am–2pm | **Tip** Fighting fires is hungry work, so if you're feeling peckish, you can visit Restaurant Sankt Peder, on Sankt Peders Vej 2, the road that runs parallel to Hellerupvej. They serve a traditional Danish lunch with herring, cheese and open-faced sandwiches.

47__The Green Courtyard
Space for healing

What are you supposed to do with an outdated hospital from 1757, when all the staff and patients have been moved to a shiny new one? They were faced with this conundrum in 1910, when it was time to close down King Frederik's Hospital (named after Frederik V, during whose reign the hospital was built), which consisted of four wards surrounding a garden, Grønnegården (The Green Courtyard). Its central location meant that it was an attractive place to rent, and it was let out to various artists until 1919, when banker Emil Glückstadt (1875–1923) bought the building. He knew exactly what to do with it – it was to house a museum dedicated to his great passion: the decorative arts. He gave it to the already established Museum of Decorative Arts, and after some refurbishments, the museum was ready to open in 1926. The museum is now the Danish Museum of Art and Design (Designmuseum Danmark), and the courtyard is an entity unto itself. The architect of the hospital, Nicolai Eigtved (1701–1754) had envisioned that the courtyard be used as a herb garden, but the doctors wanted a 'healing garden' instead.

When the hospital was turned into a museum, some of the most reputable architects of the time worked on the refurbishment, and G. N. Brandt was responsible for the garden. They all tried to encapsulate the 'spirit' of the location in their designs. Brandt removed some of the linden trees that had made the garden quite dark and dreary in grey weather. He kept the cobblestone pathway and many of the sculptures in the garden, which he rearranged in a more symmetrical fashion; these included the *Sea Horse Well* from 1916, made by the artist Niels Skovgaard (1858–1938).

King Frederik's Hospital was built to hold 300 patients, who could all go out into the garden. Even those confined to their beds would be carried out on stretchers to breathe the fresh air, and by all accounts this was a rather lively place. This 'spirit' comes back to life in the summer, when outdoor theatre performances take place there.

Address Bredgade 68, 1260 Copenhagen K, www.designmuseum.dk | **Getting there** Metro M3 to Marmorkirken | **Hours** Sun – Tue 11am – 5pm, Wed 11am – 9pm | **Tip** You can also explore the courtyards surrounding the museum. On the left-hand side is the zinc-covered Design Workshop for children.

48__Gro Spiseri

Communal dining in the thick of it

Anyone wanting to eat at Gro Spiseri (the name can be literally translated as 'Grow Eatery') needs to be quick about it. The restaurant usually sells out in a matter of minutes, and the best strategy is to subscribe to the newsletter, which lets you know when you can book a seat – you can't book a table, since everyone sits together and shares the communal platters. The food is sourced so locally that you're actually sitting among the beds where the vegetables were grown, and the eatery serves – in their own words – 'bio-hippie-rock'n'roll-gourmet-grandma-food'. Food and wine are organically and biodynamically produced, as the restaurant is part of ØsterGRO, a community-supported agricultural space whose garden farm is located high above the rooftops of Østerbro. Here, they grow organic vegetables, keep bees and chickens, and use local compost.

In 2015, ØsterGRO was the latest of several city gardens, whose purpose is both social and food-political. There are 40 member families who pay a few thousand DKK for their share of the produce, eggs and honey and for permanent access to the garden, where they can, for example, teach their children to grow vegetables. Others are welcome in the garden for workshops or markets or to lend a hand with the work, so if you can't book a seat at the eatery, you can still have a look (their Facebook page – facebook.com/farmengro – posts public events).

ØsterGRO was established by gardeners and landscape architects who are proud to say that it's the largest 'rooftop farm' in Copenhagen, at 600 square metres. Urban farming was very much in the zeitgeist, and they were given financial and practical help from a variety of organisations. Today, however, the farm is threatened by municipality laws demanding parking spaces in the area, an issue that has been under negotiation for several years. One can only hope that a solution is reached so that the farm can continue growing happily between the rooftops.

Address Æbeløgade 4, the roof, 2100 Copenhagen Ø, www.kobenhavnergron.dk/ place/ostergro | Getting there Bus 12 to Sankt Kjelds Plads | Hours Mar, Thu–Sat 5.30–8.30pm; Apr–Nov, Thu–Mon 5.30–8.30pm. You can usually visit ØsterGRO on Wed 10am–5pm in the summer and lend a hand. Groups are required to book in advance. | Tip Some other, and more accessible city gardens include Byhaven (City Garden) 2200 in Hørsholmsgade/Stefansgade by the Green Path and the Byoasen (City Oasis), Møllegade 25.

49__ The Hare Trail
Denmark's first interactive running trail

At the Children's Zoo, you can see how you compare with some of the animals – are you faster than a gazelle, a cheetah, a guinea fowl, a fox or a rabbit? In Søndermarken Park (the Southern Field) – just next to the Zoo – your challenger is the hare. Fortunately, you can pick your own speed.

The Hare Trail (its official and far less interesting name is the Fitness and Movement Trail) is 2.5 kilometres long and circles the entire park.

At the entrances Bag Søndermarken and off Roskildevej, there are large posts where you can switch the 'hare' on, choose your direction (clockwise or anticlockwise) and set your pace. Then you switch on the nearest bollard, which lights up for a few seconds before the light darts off to the next. Now all you have to do is get going and chase the 'hare' from bollard to bollard.

In addition to the motivational aspect of racing something, the lights also mean that you can run in the dark, since the bollards light your way. Along the trail you'll find four 'activity spots' where you can practise your coordination, balance and strength, do plyometric training, circuit training and finally stretch out.

The trail is part of a larger project that ran in Søndermarken until 2013. The idea was to combine nature with culture and exercise. As well as the trail, the historical elements of the park were renovated or recreated, and former wetlands were re-established, such as the canals called Siberia. Information points with QR codes were also set up around the park, so you can learn more while walking around.

Whether you're out for a run or taking a more leisurely stroll, Søndermarken Park is a wonderful place to explore. It is slightly more hilly and rough than its neighbour Frederiksberg Gardens, with old trees (some of them home to owls!) and large open spaces which often host concerts or sports events in the summer months.

Address Søndermarken, 2000 Frederiksberg | Getting there For the Roskildevej entrance: Bus 7A, 18, 26, 72 to De små haver; for the Bag Søndermarken entrance: Bus 18, 26 to Gammel Jernbanevej | Tip In Søndermarken, just across from the entrance to the zoo, you can visit the cisterns under the park, where there are now art exhibitions (cisternerne.dk/en).

50 The Harbour Buses

Copenhagen's newest buildings from a different angle

Building cranes rarely stand idle in Copenhagen. If you want the best view of the latest developments in the city, we recommend that you take the harbour bus from north to south.

On the way south from Refshaleøen, you can enjoy – or be outraged at – the Opera House from 2005. It was designed by world-famous architect Henning Larsen and has been the subject of heated debates among Copenhageners. On the opposite side, you'll find the new Playhouse from 2008 by Lundgaard and Tranberg Architects, and just past the Langebro Bridge is the Black Diamond, a modern expansion of the Royal Library designed by Schmidt Hammer Lassen Architects.

Past the library, on Kalvebod Brygge, you can see a stretch of office buildings from the 1990s. These have been much maligned for not only being ugly, but also cutting off the view of the harbour. In recent years, the municipal company By & Havn (Town and Harbour) has been working tirelessly to reopen the area with projects such as Kalvebod Waves by the Langebro bridge, and the labour union IDA runs a café outside its headquarters in the summer.

Further south – by the Bryggebroen Bridge – there are new buildings, for better or worse. There are some beautiful apartments, such as the white ones with offset balconies (also by Lundgaard and Tranberg), but unfortunately there are also some buildings that might make one wonder whether the architect was on holiday when they were designed.

After Bryggebroen, you can see the H. C. Ørsted Power Station from 1920 and Enghave Brygge, which used to be a part of the industrial harbour but is now being turned into housing, commercial buildings and recreational areas under the name Frederiks Brygge.

The final stop on the harbour bus is Teglholmen, where you can get off and take a walk around the nearby Sluseholmen with its Amsterdam-inspired architecture (see ch. 91).

Route Refshaleøen – Nordre Toldbod – Holmen Nord – The Opera House – Nyhavn – Knippelsbro Bridge – The Royal Library – Bryggeholmen – Teglholmen | Getting there Harbour Bus 991, 992 from one of the stops listed above | Tip Take a walk or bike ride along the harbour – you can use the bridges to cross back and forth and follow the waterfront all the way through the city.

51　Helgoland Baths

A cornerstone of civilisation

In the past, any self-respecting metropolis simply had to have one or more public baths. It was a way to provide the opportunity for good hygiene to people who didn't have bathrooms at home, and this is why the City ran a number of bathhouses like the one in Sjællandsgade (see ch. 90).

But bathhouses weren't enough; outdoor bathing facilities were also required – not just for the poor, who couldn't afford the bathhouses, but for anyone who wanted to take in the fresh air, sunlight and clean water in civilised, partitioned surroundings. Not to be outdone by other major coastal cities, Copenhagen also wanted an outdoor bath, and salt importer A. W. Colding (1861–1919) initiated the building of a sea bath at Svanemøllen Bay in 1910. It was named after the German island Helgoland, which at that time was known for its mild climate, sandy beaches and health spas.

The clean water didn't last long though – a few years later, a sewer line was directed into the bay and Helgoland was forced to move to Amager.

This did not harm the popularity of the baths, which have gained an iconic status among many Copenhageners. Many residents of Amager (or Amagricans, as they like to be called) over the age of 40 presumably took their first swim in the baths, where swimming lessons were given until the 1970s. The baths are still in use, even though Helgoland is now just a small part of the larger Amager Beach Park complex, where most bathers go directly into the water from the beach.

The Helgoland Baths are also famous for their winter bathers. A society called Det Kolde Gys (The Cold Shiver) has been based in Helgoland since 1929, and membership of the society is required if you want to bathe here in the winter or use the saunas, which come in handy in the cold! Winter bathing is a popular activity in Denmark, and 'the Shiver' has more than 2,000 paying members.

Address Øresundsstien 11, 2300 Copenhagen S | Getting there Metro M2 to Øresund | Hours 23 June–31 Aug, 10am–6pm | Tip From Helgoland, you can see the little marina belonging to Sundby Yacht Club. Here you can visit the Maritime Youth Centre, whose wavy deck is worth the trip, as well as Restaurant Sundby Sejl, which serves high-quality traditional Danish cuisine in charming surroundings.

52 Hellerup Beach Park

Bathing and barbecuing

The Beach Park (Strandpark) in Hellerup is a reflection of leisure activities as they were just before the outbreak of the First World War, when functionality had begun to encroach on the purely decorative. While there may still be a perennial garden and a rose garden, there is also a beach, tennis courts and a marina.

The man responsible for it all, landscape gardener G. N. Brandt (1878–1945), left his mark on a number of public and private gardens, parks and cemeteries throughout the country. Many of them are in Copenhagen (such as Grønnegården, see ch. 47, and the Parterre Gardens in Tivoli) but Brandt was first and foremost responsible for a plethora of parks in Gentofte, among others the Øregaard Park (see ch. 77). He was the great inspiration for a generation of landscape gardeners who were active after the Second World War.

Brandt created a symmetrical rose garden laid out around an axis leading out towards Øresund, with 40 different types of roses in many different colours. They're planted so that the palest roses are closest to the sea, and they become yellow, pink, orange and deep red as they go further inland.

The perennial garden, containing approximately 100 different species, is also laid out symmetrically, with the flowerbeds circling a lawn – something quite unheard of in 1912. The grass is now so popular among sunbathers that the City has had to create more paths through the flowerbeds. Parks are used quite differently today than they were in Brandt's time, when you weren't allowed on the grass, and even the rose garden has had to succumb to the anarchy of modern life. People can sit and barbecue here, or lean back carelessly against the sandstone vases, thought to originally come from Amalienborg Palace. Children can also play on the little playground, where modern landscape architects have taken elements from the marina and created a jetty that goes out to a 'pool' of blue rubber.

Address Onsgårdsvej / Strandparkvej, 2900 Hellerup | **Getting there** Bus 23, 171, 172 to Onsgårdsvej | **Tip** There is an app called Badevand that allows you to check the temperature of the water before getting too excited about going in.

53 Hellerup Marina

A yacht club with Olympic aspirations

It's located at 55° 43.9' N – 12° 35' E if you're travelling by boat, and it's off Strandvejen if you arrive by bus (go by Onsgårdsvej or Strandparksvej). The marina (*lystbådehavn*) is part of a larger beach park organised along neoclassicist lines, where each section has its own features, such as the flower gardens, playground, tennis courts and docks, which were built in 1911 and form the centre of the park.

The park and the marina are two separate entities, with the park being open to all, while the marina is mainly for members of the Hellerup Sejlklub / Yacht Club, which celebrated its 100th anniversary in 2015. It has over 1,000 members, making it one of the largest in Denmark, and it has many long-standing traditions. The members of the club have won a total of 13 Olympic medals so far, and it counts Danish legend and four-time Olympic gold medallist Paul Elvstrøm among its members. In 2015, the club was proclaimed the sixth most successful yacht club in Europe.

The Yacht Club offers a wide selection of training for its junior and senior members, including Optimist and Feva dinghies for beginners, as stepping stones on the path to a 'real' dinghy. The next step might be one of the club 29ers, chosen by young sailors training for the somewhat bigger, two-handed 49ers – high-performance sailing dinghies, which have been competing at the Olympics since 2000.

No decent yacht club is complete without a restaurant, and this one has Restaurant Hellerup Sejlklub, which advertises Danish cuisine such as open rye sandwiches and the classic 'shooting star', a creation of plaice fillet, shrimp and asparagus. The restaurant also offers a stunning view of the sea from the rooftop terrace. From here you can see traces of the flooding caused by the terrible storm Bodil, which hit Denmark in 2014. Safety measures taken after the storm do, sadly, block some of the view from the beach.

Address Onsgårdsvej / Strandparkvej, 2900 Hellerup | Getting there Bus 23, 171, 172 to Onsgårdsvej | Tip If you walk around the boat house towards Frederikkevej and go parallel to the coast, you'll hit Carolinevej and then the path leading to Tuborg Havn (where the famous Danish beer was once brewed) and on to Svanemøllen Beach Svaneknoppen (see ch. 102).

54 Imam Ali Mosque
A landmark of northwestern Copenhagen

The northwestern part of Copenhagen has a new landmark. Two towers and a turquoise dome rise up among the houses in the 'bird quarter' and can help you successfully navigate the many seemingly identical streets, all of them named after birds.

The towers are minarets and the dome sits on top of the city's first Shia mosque, which opened in 2015. The mosque on Vibevej (Lapwing Street) has a distinctive Middle Eastern feel to it, with floral tiles of turquoise and midnight blue, and ornaments adorning the walls, on which there are calligraphic verses from the Quran along with their Danish translations. There's also marble – enormous amounts of it have been used in both the floors and walls. Worried about getting cold feet here in these northern climes? Don't worry, they've installed under-floor heating.

The mosque was many years in the making and has sparked some debate in Denmark. Can a Christian country like Denmark, with churches on every hilltop, deal with a mosque – and a mosque with minarets at that? The debate died down and it was decided that Denmark was big enough for a mosque, and so the building began – fortunately, for the result is beautiful.

In addition to several prayer rooms, the mosque has a conference hall, meeting rooms, guest rooms, youth centre, offices and parking. The central dome has space for 1,500 people, and the minarets are 32 metres tall. Then there's the kitchen, which is said to be equipped to serve 5,000 people!

You're welcome to come by and have a look during the week, and the mosque really is worth looking at. But do be respectful of those at prayer, especially during services and sermons. Sundays are official visiting days, where volunteers give tours of the mosque and talk about life as a Danish Muslim. Please remember to dress appropriately: cover your shoulders and knees, and it is most appreciated if women cover their heads.

Address Vibevej 25–27, 2400 Copenhagen NV, www.imamalimoske.dk, facebook.com/intmuswor | Getting there Bus 4C to Frederikssundsvej; bus 5C, 4A, 250S, 350S, 12; bus 5C, 4A, 250S, 350S, 12; Metro M3 or S-train F to Nørrebro | Hours First Sundays of the month, 2pm (for a free tour) | Tip The first Sunni mosque in Copenhagen opened in 2014 in Nørrebro. Its official name is the Hamad Bin Khalifa Civilisation Centre, but it's usually just known as the Great Mosque. Its architecture is more Nordic than that of the Imam Ali Mosque.

55 __ Israel's Square

A climate-friendly flying carpet

Who hasn't wished for a flying carpet at one time or another? Surely that would be something to cherish! When you look at the children running around the so-called flying carpet on Copenhagen's Israel's Square, you're certain that they do appreciate it. Sadly, this is not Aladdin, but it's the next best thing.

The southern part of Israel's Square was given a complete overhaul between 2013 and 2014 by COBE Architects, who were also responsible for the public library on Rentemestervej (see ch. 63), and Sweco Landscape Architects. They've made the square float 30 centimetres above the ground! The carpet creases at the southwestern and northeastern corners, creating steps from which you can watch the world go by or have a chat with your friends. The border running along the outside of the square lights up at night and enhances the flying carpet effect.

The carpet invites children on all kinds of wheels to play and exercise here, but it's also used for street food and flea markets, as a picnic area and as a general hang-out spot. There's also an area for ballgames, a playground, a skating ramp and lots of benches under the trees. The idea is to let the adjacent Ørstedsparken 'encroach' on the city through the trees. While the granite on the carpet's surface may seem somewhat cold and harsh, once the trees have grown, their crowns will create a cosier atmosphere and the border between the park and the square will be practically gone.

Like at the City Dune (see ch. 88), the effects of the changing climate have been incorporated into the design. At the southwestern corner, there's a little stream with small fountains created by sculptor Morten Stræde. Under the square is a 40-cubic-metre water tank, which fills up with rainwater that feeds into the 80-metre-long stream. There are stepping stones in the stream, so children and other adventurous types can jump across, and on the border to the park it becomes a waterfall.

Address Israel's Square, 1361 Copenhagen K | Getting there Bus 5C, 6A, 150S, 14, 184, 185; Metro M1, M2 or S-train A, B, Bx, C, E, H to Nørreport | Tip On Fridays and Saturdays from April to October there are flea markets on Israel's Square between 9am and 4pm.

56__ J. C. Jacobsen's Garden (The Academy Garden)

A breath of fresh air between old beer and a new brewery

This old brewer's garden is perhaps the most secret patch of grass in Copenhagen, and as a result it's rarely crowded. It's hidden among all the other attractions at the old Carlsberg brewery, including the Visit Carlsberg Centre.

Once you've found your way past the Dance Theatre, you can almost feel yourself leaving the big city behind as you move closer to green tranquillity.

The whole Carlsberg area is currently undergoing massive reconstruction, so there are cranes and diggers everywhere, and although they can be seen from the garden, all the noise – from them as well as the trains and cars below – somehow fades away as you walk through the garden with its exotic trees, little pond and abundance of flowers and bushes.

The garden looks its best in late spring or during the summer, when everything is in bloom. The tree stump in the middle is the perfect place to take in everything around you. But the garden is certainly worth visiting when covered in winter snow as well.

You can walk up to the gate leading into Carlsberg's beautiful Honorary Residence, built in 1853. You can't go in, but fortunately it's quite striking from afar. You might even be lucky enough to see the draught horses grazing next door. Please don't feed them, but it's worth having a look, especially if you have children. From here, you can go into the thicket and down to the little pond, and end your trip at the red-brick wall from 1969 where the bricks are placed at an angle, sticking their tips out and creating an intricate pattern. The old buildings behind the wall are being torn down, but the wall has been allowed to stay.

If the sun's out, the garden's the perfect place to bring a blanket and a good book, or perhaps a group of friends and some cold beer.

Address Pasteursvej, 1778 Copenhagen V (find the path behind the Dance Theatre) | **Getting there** Bus 1A, 9A, 10 or S-train B, Bx, C, H to Carlsberg | **Tip** There's much more to see in the Carlsberg area, including the Elephant Gate, and various places to eat and – of course – drink.

57 Jægersborggade

A street with style and substance

The street has, indirectly, the construction magnate Kay Wilhelmsen to thank for its famous (both at home and abroad) small, specialist shops, cafés and restaurants. Among them are the ultra-hip restaurant Grød ('Porridge' – guess what they serve), the Michelin-starred restaurant Relæ, the Coffee Collective (which works to secure better standards of living for coffee farmers), and a bakery owned by Claus Meyer (one of the founders of Noma), whose aim is to heighten the quality of Danish food culture.

The shops have very different styles, but they share a lot of the same values. Many state that they want to set new standards, and that they care deeply about ecology – whether it be meat or vegetables.

Wilhelmsen was known for his spectacular projects and his equally spectacular bankruptcies. One of his companies bought up most of the street at a time when it was derelict and run by motorcycle gangs and drug dealers, with the intention of rebuilding it. When the company went bankrupt in 1992, the residents of Jægersborggade were given the option to buy their buildings from the insolvent company, and the association AB Jæger came into being. It consists of 49 apartment buildings and most ground-floor and basement properties are rented out to shops, preferably ones that are open more than 40 hours a week.

This can't, of course, explain the special feel of the street, with its variety of shops. Before the credit crunch in 2008, most of the ground-floor and basement properties were used as storage or parking for bicycles, but little shops and restaurants started popping up all over the street and the neighbouring Stefansgade. It could be that young people and students were forced to stay in the neighbourhood, or perhaps entrepreneurs eyed the possibility to carve out a new market in this blossoming neighbourhood. Either way, Jægersborggade has proven the Danish saying that no situation is so bad that it isn't good for something.

Address Jægersborggade, 2200 Copenhagen N, www.jaegersborggade.com | Getting there Bus 18 to Jægersborggade; bus 68 or Metro M3 to Nuuks Plads; bus 5C, 350S or Metro M3 to Nørrebros Runddel | Hours Most shops Mon–Fri 10am–6pm, Sat 10am–4pm | Tip The large supervised playground in the nearby Nørrebro Park has a paddling pool, areas for ballgames and a shed for playing inside.

58 Kayak Republic and Kayak Bar

The boating republic by Knippelsbro Bridge

Copenhagen is equal parts water and land. If not in area, then at least in the consciousness of Copenhageners. In the 20 years since the South Harbour was closed down as an industrial harbour, there has been a boom in recreational opportunities by the waterfront. Kayaks, canoes, rowing and speedboats now rule the waves, and at Kayak Republic you can book kayaking trips with an instructor, affording you not only a kayaking experience, but also a different sightseeing trip through Copenhagen.

You could turn up for the 10am City Tour, for example, where you spend two hours paddling out to *The Little Mermaid* on Langelinie and back again through the canals of Christianshavn. You can also book other tours or hire a single kayak and go out on your own (children under 18 must be accompanied by an adult). You can borrow wetsuits and other gear, or bring your own.

The Republic is somewhat hidden along the side of Knippelsbro Bridge – if you don't know it's there, you could easily miss it. But if you pause to enjoy the view from the north side of the bridge, look down – the kayak rental and the palm trees in the Kayak Bar will be teeming with people.

If you prefer enjoying the water from afar, the Kayak Bar is the place for you. The view of Holmen Church and Christiansborg Palace Church is as picturesque as they get. You'll also come to see why Copenhagen is known as a city of towers, as the spires of the Church of the Holy Spirit and St Nicholas Church gleam in the sunlight. The tower of the Church of Our Lady is seen in all its classicist splendour, while the Church of Our Saviour winds up towards the heavens.

The Kayak Bar is open all year round and there are often concerts held here. It's a popular place, and you can't book a table, so take your chances and pop by.

Address Børskaj 12, 1221 Copenhagen K, www.kayakrepublic.dk, kayakbar.dk | Getting there Bus 2A, 31, 37 to Børsen | Tip Drop in at Kayak Republic at the feast of St Lucia on 13 December. The traditional candlelight procession gets a kayak-style makeover.

59 The Kiosk at Kultorvet

An inner-city garden pavilion

In Persian they call them *ūš kūsh*, in Turkish *kiösk* or *köšk*, and the word originally – in the Ottoman Empire – meant a decorated garden pavilion. The Ottoman pavilion was the direct inspiration for pavilions in the 18th-century romantic gardens of many European countries, and it was the model for the larger musical pavilions which spread all over Europe. In Paris, the kiosk, *le kiosque*, was brought in for the new boulevards in the mid-19th century as a place to sell newspapers, and by the 1890s the kiosk had made it to Copenhagen as a kind of combined newsstand and phone box. It's this kind of kiosk that can still be seen on Kultorvet today – although now it's used for outdoor serving.

About 20 of these kiosks were put up on squares all around town, in addition to a couple of somewhat larger octagonal kiosks, like the one found on The King's Square (Kongens Nytorv). The bigger model was never a success with the public, nor with the company who produced them, which preferred the smaller hexagonal type created by architect Fritz Koch (1857–1905). It has a copper roof as if it were a Gothic spire, with clocks on three sides, and under the roof are Viking-style woodcarvings depicting, among other things, the 12 signs of the zodiac. The base is of granite, and the large windows are meant for displaying advertisements, not for letting light in, as the kiosk also served as a sort of manned advertising column.

The last of Koch's kiosks was put up as late as 1928 on Sankt Hans Square (see ch. 97). That was the end of the decorated kiosks, which were replaced by newsstands and telephone boxes in the functionalist style of the time. This was before the telephone was a common household item. As more and more people had phones put in and their papers delivered to their homes, the kiosks became rather obsolete. In 1980, the firm that produced the kiosks was forced to close down, but many of the pretty little kiosks still remain in the city and now have various purposes.

Address Kultorvet, 1175 Copenhagen K | Getting there Bus 5C, 6A, 150S, 14, 184, 185; Metro M1, M2 or S-train A, B, Bx, C, E, H to Nørreport | Tip Nørreport station is close to Kultorvet. It is the busiest in Denmark, serving S-trains, metro and regional trains. It has recently been rebuilt, but is still one of the most hectic places in the city – it's just slightly more appealing than before.

60 Kjær & Sommerfeldt
Wine merchant in grandiose surroundings

Without the sign above the door stating this is a 'Purveyor to the Court of Denmark' (*Kgl. Hof Vinhandler*), you might think it was an old-fashioned public office (and in fact it was originally meant to be a telegraph office). It never was, however, and now you can rejoice at the sight of an outstanding wine merchant's, which was furnished in 1928 with a rare Poul Henningsen chandelier as its focal point.

The wine merchant's was founded in 1875, and appointed Purveyor to the Court of Denmark in 1901, at a time when special titles such as Royal Fishmonger, Royal Photographer, Royal Jeweller (such as P. Hertz, see ch. 78) and even a Royal Wax Flower Seller were given out. Nowadays, people can apply for a royal warrant of appointment, allowing them to display this appointment and use a crown in their signage and letterheads, and there are approximately 100 such purveyors in Denmark today. The court reports that they receive roughly 10 applications a year, and applicants can wait for several years before hearing back.

The interiors of Kjær & Sommerfeldt haven't changed much since the company moved into its current location in 1928 to sell liquors, cigars, wine and champagne. The only major difference is that the original cigar area has been turned into a wine bar – but not just any old wine bar. It's presented as a fancy historical dispensary and was furnished by two anthropologists, using furniture and other things from company storage. Here you can join the weekly wine bar on Fridays and Saturdays, or participate in themed monthly wine tastings. Once a year, the company hosts a charity bar on behalf of a non-profit organisation benefitting children, where anyone who's anyone turns up to bask in the light of the chandelier, lounge on the balcony or stand outside, all of course holding a glass of wine. This is how they managed to raise 74,000 DKK in 2015 for a charity that – perhaps somewhat ironically – aids children whose parents have drinking problems.

Address Gammel Mønt 4, 1117 Copenhagen K, www.kogs.dk | Getting there Bus 23 or Metro M 1, M 2, M 3 to Kongens Nytorv | Hours Mon – Thu 10am – 6pm, Fri 10am – 8pm, Sat 11am – 7pm | Tip The Cinematheque is close by and hosts film festivals, shows classic or forgotten films, and even Danish films subtitled in English on Sundays. There's a restaurant Sult ('Hunger'), a library and a bookshop. See dfi.dk/Service/English.

61_Kringlegangen
Between the bustle of Strøget and the calm of the square

In 1975, a passage was made which led from Valkendorfgade by the Church of the Holy Spirit (Helligåndskirken) on Strøget (the shopping street) to Grey Friar's Square. It was given the name Kringlegangen (the Convoluted Alley) due to its twists and turns. Names ending in 'gangen' (the Danish word for hallway) had historically been given to very narrow streets inside the city walls.

Poorhouses were often to be found in these narrow streets, but they were also favoured by prostitutes. The majority were removed during redevelopments around the beginning of the 20th century. They were later re-established as a combination of passages and commercial properties, such as Sankt Petri Passage, between Nørregade and Larslejsstræde, and Klostergangen (Convent Alley), on the other side of the Church of the Holy Spirit, leading to Kompagnistræde, which were both opened in the 1920s.

Kringlegangen was introduced in the 1970s, when there was a desire to recreate some of the historical urban spaces that had been demolished in the past century. This is also why you can still marvel at the various 17th- and 18th-century houses on Grey Friar's Square, which had been used as a bomb shelter during the Second World War, and a car park until 1968. The only redeeming quality the square had at that time was the big plane tree from 1904, which grew nicely there, as it was once a cemetery when the square was a Franciscan monastery. By the time of the Reformation in the 16th century, the monks were gone and a nobleman had built his estate on the site. He was later sentenced to death for treason in absentia and, as he wasn't around to be punished, they tore down his house and laid down the square instead.

In the 1970s and 1980s, Grey Friar's Square was one of the town's hot spots, and people would sit in large groups on the cobblestones. These days, people convene in other places, such as Queen Louise's Bridge (see ch. 84), so you can usually find a place to sit underneath the plane tree.

Address Valkendorfsgade 32 and Grey Friar's Square 17, 1154 Copenhagen K | Getting there Bus 2A, 23, 32, 37 or Metro M3 to Gammel Strand | Tip The Church of the Holy Spirit, with entrances from both Strøget and Valkendorfsgade, is one of the oldest buildings in Copenhagen and there is almost always something going on, such as art exhibitions, a Christmas market or a second-hand book sale, where the books are sold in the style of a 'Dutch auction', where prices are lowered day by day.

62 The Lapidarium of Kings
A home for retired statues

It's not just big, or even enormous; the statue of King Frederik V in Amalienborg Palace Square is simply gigantic. You probably won't even notice as you stand next to it, since it's high up on its pedestal. But at the Lapidarium of Kings you can see that you only come up to the horse's knees, and have to tilt your head well back to be able to see the laurel wreath on the king's head, five metres above you. Once you've adjusted to its size, you have the opportunity to study in detail this plaster copy of one of the five most splendid equestrian statues in the world.

The Lapidarium of Kings exhibits original statues and carvings from the royal castles and palaces of Denmark. The sculptures – most of them from the late 18th century – have been stored here because centuries of having been subjected to wind, rain and pollution meant that they were looking rather worse for wear. New versions are therefore made to replace the original statues, and the old ones are hidden away in storage along with the plaster casts of the new ones.

But why should these beautiful objects just sit and collect dust for no reason?

This must be what the Agency for Culture and Palaces thought when they decided to open the Lapidarium as an indoor museum, where the sculptures are protected from the elements. Two birds with one stone, as it were, since it also meant that people could now gain access to King Christian IV's listed brewery, which provides a splendid home for the sculptures.

You begin your journey in the casemate (on the ground floor), which features original statues from the royal palace at Fredensborg (north of Copenhagen) and the equestrian statues, including the original lead statue of Christian VI from Kongens Nytorv, which was replaced with a bronze replica in 1946. On the first floor you'll find capitals, pediments and plants carved in stone, and even a statue of the ancient world's strongest man, Hercules.

Address Christian IV's Bryghus, Frederiksholms Kanal 29, 1220 Copenhagen K, www.kongerneslapidarium.dk | Getting there Bus 26 to Det Kongelige Bibliotek; bus 2A, 23, 31, 37 to Stormbroen/Nationalmuseet | Hours July, Tue–Sun noon–4pm (guided tours can be booked all year) | Tip *Lapis* is the Latin word for stone, and a lapidarium is therefore a place containing stones (in the way an aquarium contains water).

63 The Library on Rentemestervej

Liberty and culture for all

On Tomsgårdsvej, you'll find two large houses back to back: the public library (official name: Biblioteket) resplendent with its bronzed exterior, and the rebellious Youth House (Ungdomshuset) covered in graffiti. However, more connects these two houses than just their location – the library owes its existence to the Youth House, as it was built as compensation for moving the Youth House to the area.

The new Youth House opened in the autumn of 2008 and the library followed in 2011. The architects who designed the building were also responsible for the interiors, which are some of the more advanced and innovative among the public libraries in Copenhagen. The children's library, for instance, is built for climbing around in. The library also contains creative workshops, citizens' services, conference rooms and local TV and radio stations. There's also Café Glad, which – very much in tune with the zeitgeist – focuses on organic seasonal produce.

The library is first and foremost a library, of course, but it's very aware of its location in one of the more socially challenged neighbourhoods of Copenhagen. It therefore offers many activities for children and young people during the summer holidays, and provides after-school homework programmes, as well as offering a number of services, including economic and legal advice.

Both the outside and inside are decorated by the artist Husk-MitNavn (RememberMyName) who painted illegal graffiti in the 1990s, but by 2001 had become an established street artist with exhibitions around the world and an extensive social media following. However, he remains just as anonymous as the frequenters of the Youth House, with whom the library also engages (e.g. at the yearly carnival, where they're invited to join in the festivities and eat vegan cream buns).

Address Rentemestervej 76, 2400 Copenhagen NV, www.bibliotek.kk.dk/bibliotek/
rentemestervej | Getting there Bus 5C, 250S, 21 to Hulgårds Plads, 21 to Birkedommervej |
Hours Mon–Fri 1am–6pm, Sat 11am–2pm | Tip Just around the corner on Tomsgårdsvej
23C you'll find Hammam & Spa Copenhagen, where you can enjoy a traditional Turkish
bath and massage or perhaps a ghassoul facial.

64 The Library in Tingbjerg
A type case of activity

The new library in Tingbjerg is abuzz with children. Both during the afternoon and in the evening, kids of all ages run around playing or sit leafing through books, while adults make use of the many cosy nooks set up for holding meetings, doing homework or simply having a chat. It's generally at its liveliest during the day, as the library functions as an extension of Tingbjerg School with about 500 pupils, so the workshops and playrooms are understandably busy.

Tingbjerg is currently on the official list of Danish ghetto areas, but it's hoped that the library will be a new, positive symbol of the neighbourhood and help counter some of the stigma it has experienced. It would certainly have been possible to construct a more ordinary-looking building, and probably one that was cheaper than the 58 million DKK that this one has cost. But when the great transformation of the area began in 2000, the residents behind it wanted something special – and something not built in the yellow brick of all other public structures in Tingbjerg! It did admittedly end up with yellow brick, but the building got to stand out in all other respects: It's quite a bit taller than everything else (with the exception of a single high-rise), and its shape is very different. It almost looks like half a pyramid, 18 metres at its highest point and 1.5 at its lowest. Inside, it seemingly consists of a single, large room with the various floors set in as staggered balconies; the interior is inspired by the traditional wooden type cases that typographers once used. Everything appears light and fragile, but don't be fooled by the wooden panelling: behind it is solid concrete.

So far it's impossible to tell whether the new library can counteract the area's ghetto stigma, but there's no doubt about its positive role. Recently its oldest employee celebrated 25 years in the job, and said in a speech that he'd once spent hours daily telling noisy children off – until he'd realised that he'd just have to activate them. The new library building presents plenty of opportunities for that.

Address Skolesiden 4, 2700 Brønshøj, bibliotek.kk.dk/bibliotek/tingbjerg | Getting there Bus 2A, 132 to Tingbjerg Skole | Hours Mon–Thu 2–6pm, Fri 2–5pm, Sat 10am–2pm. Staff and opening hours may vary. | Tip A short walk away, on Terrasserne 40, the Tingbjerg School runs a playground petting zoo. Here are horses, rabbits, chickens, budgies and pot-bellied pigs – but remember to talk to the staff before you go to pet the animals.

65 Løvenborg
Art nouveau on Vesterbro

The façade is richly decorated in (almost) real sandstone and copper ribbons with gilded floral decorations, and on the cornice at the top it says *Løvenborg* (Lion Castle) in a kind of escutcheon. However, this is only due to the fact that there used to be a bar here by that name. Although its decorations are fit for a king, the house was built as an office building with a seamstress in the attic, a cinema on the ground floor and the Hotel Savoy in the rear wing. Today, only the hotel remains.

Løvenborg was designed by Anton Rosen (1859–1928), one of the few Danish architects to design buildings in pure Jugendstil or art nouveau style (see ch. 70). The building was completed in 1906, but was on the verge of collapse in the 1980s. It was saved by the Dreyer Foundation, which now has offices in the building and has had part of it turned into housing for visiting lecturers at the School of Architecture.

The foundation was established by architect Torvald Dreyer and solicitor Margot Dreyer in 1976, and each year it awards close to 20 million DKK to 'projects and research stays benefitting the judicial or architectural professions'.

The money comes from the assets the couple amassed through building projects in Copenhagen. As an architect, Dreyer was responsible for rather anonymous concrete or brick houses built with little regard to their surroundings. It's therefore a kind of historic irony that Dreyer's foundation should work out of this building, as Rosen had a very different approach. His houses were exotic, and characterised by good craftsmanship, high-quality materials and copious amounts of decoration. The design of Løvenborg was innovative to boot, with its use of a new technique, the 'curtain wall', where the façade is pre-made and hung on the construction. Sadly, the house can only be admired from the outside, but you can stay in the Hotel Savoy, away from the street noise.

Address Vesterbrogade 34, 1620 Copenhagen V | Getting there Bus 7A to Vesterbros Torv | Tip Take a moment to enjoy the cafés on Vesterbro Square (Vesterbro Torv), from which you can walk further into Vesterbro and Frederiksberg via, for example, Værnedamsvej, which is full of little cafés and boutiques.

66 Lygten Station
*Stand-up comedy and heavy metal in
National Romantic surroundings*

Lygten Station looks rather closed and abandoned compared to the multitude of people and shops in Nørrebro during the day. But at night – that's when it really comes alive with an underground cinema, stand-up comedy and concerts, because Lygten is more than a station – it's a venue. It's especially popular among stand-up comedians, both established and up-and-coming. It also offers English-language comedy (including improv comedy shows), as well as monthly film screenings and various concerts, some connected to the yearly heavy metal festival Copenhell. Check the calendar on the website for information about upcoming events. Lygten seats roughly 70 people in the former station building, making it perfect for intimate performances.

The station is on the boundary between the Nørrebro and North-West neighbourhoods. Until 1901, it was the border of the Municipality of Copenhagen, marked by the nearby stream which is now dried up. The station was built in 1905, and the trains would go to Nordsjælland (Northern Zealand) and were often used by people going on picnics, because they would take you straight to the large Hareskoven Forest. In 1976, the line was discontinued and the station was closed, and it has since been used for a number of things – just as it is today. If you'd like to see what it looks like on the inside without attending a performance, you can go to Østerport Station or Central Station, as they were designed by the same architect, Heinrich Wenck (1851–1936), who designed around 150 other stations in the 40 years he worked for the Danish State Railway. Many of them were built in the same National Romantic style, with elements from the Italian Renaissance and some Viking Age thrown in for good measure.

A little way further down the street is Lygtens Kro (The Lygten Inn), a fixture of the neighbourhood and a great place to grab a beer.

Address Lygten 2, 2400 Copenhagen NV, www.lygtenstation.dk | Getting there Bus 4A, 5C, 250S, 350S, 12; Metro M3 or S-train F to Nørrebro | Tip You can find the street food market Verdenshjørnet (World Corner) right across the street (Tue–Sun 11.30am–9.30pm).

67 __Magstræde

In the oldest part of Copenhagen

The history of Copenhagen is full of significant dates. Take the 1640s for instance, the decade in which the house at Magstræde 17–19 was built. Or 1728, when most of Copenhagen burned to the ground, but number 17–19 was mercifully spared from the fames.

Another noteworthy year was 1795, when the city was once again in flames. On this occasion, all of the southern side (with the uneven house numbers) of Magstræde survived. How about 1807, when Copenhagen was bombed by the English because Denmark had joined sides with France in the Napoleonic Wars. The bombs never reached Magstræde.

That's why you'll find the oldest parts of Copenhagen here. The house at number 17–19 from the 1640s is among the oldest in the city, as most medieval buildings were lost in the fire of 1728.

Magstræde still feels like old Copenhagen. The street is small and slightly curved, and the old houses lean slightly to one side and often into the street. Not to mention the cobblestones and minimal pavements – you'd best leave your stilettos at home!

The word '*mag*' means latrine, and the name dates back to when the area was home to the public Western Mag (the Eastern Mag was in Hyskenstræde – '*hysken*' also means latrine). In medieval times, the shoreline came up to around here, and the Copenhageners would do their business as close to the water – and as far away from residential areas – as possible. In the 1520s, the shoreline was moved further away, and the public latrine was removed and Magstræde actually became a rather fancy address.

In the late 19th century, the street became one of several official 'brothel streets' during the time of regulated prostitution, where prostitutes were allowed to work provided they were registered and submitted to regular check-ups. Nowadays, it's very hip and houses Gorm's Gourmet Pizza, one of the most popular restaurants in Copenhagen at the moment.

Address Magstræde, 1204 Copenhagen K | Getting there Bus 2A, 23, 31, 37 to Stormbroen / Nationalmuseet | Tip Huset KBH (in Rådhusstræde 13) houses the Bastard Café (a must for fans for board games), the restaurant Rub & Stub (which only serves food made from surplus food donated from shops and restaurants), as well as a cinema, theatre and concert venue.

68 The Meatpacking District
From hanging meat to hanging out

Big open spaces, concrete floors, meat hooks in the ceilings and shiny tiles on the walls, making it easy to clean off blood or other waste associated with butchery. Many people must have shaken their heads at the idea of turning the former butcher stalls and abattoirs of Kødbyen (literally 'Meat City') into the city's newest recreational district, full of bars, nightclubs and restaurants. Yet even the most sceptical came round to the idea in the end.

The Meatpacking District consists of three areas named after the predominant colour of their buildings: Grey, Brown and White. The White part was established in 1934 and was designed for food production, and it was no great jump from preparing the meat to serving it when Kødbyen became the restaurant hub it is today.

Kødbyen is a kind of oasis in the middle of Copenhagen. As soon as you turn the corner into Slagterboderne (Butcher Stalls) or Høkerboderne (Hawker Stalls), you're in a different world, an area that, since the mid-2000s, has been the place to see and be seen. A few shops still remain: a fishmonger's, a wholesale supermarket and a shop selling kitchenware to both businesses and private individuals. They all contribute to the authenticity of Kødbyen, as you peruse the many bars and restaurants.

The smell of barbecued meat and freshly poured draught beer hangs in the air. Carlsberg and Tuborg are dirty words here, as beer should preferably be from domestic or foreign microbreweries. The restaurants specialise in fusion cuisine, using the best ingredients possible, with meat, fish and poultry often dominating the menus. The quality is high, and the prices are manageable, though hardly cheap, and the raw and rustic design of the buildings is maintained everywhere. This seems to appeal to the public, who descend on Kødbyen in great numbers. The restaurants are usually packed all week, and on Friday and Saturday nights, the bars turn into a veritable meat market – so some things never change!

Address Flæsketorvet, Høkerboderne, Kødboderne, Slagterboderne, 1711, 1712, 1714, 1716, Copenhagen V | Getting there Bus 23 to Gasværksvej; bus 10 or S-train A, B, Bx, C, E, H to Dybbølsbro | Tip Not far from Kødbyen – on the corner of Sønder Boulevard and Skelbækgade – you'll find the bar Fermentoren. It's worth a visit if you're interested in good and varied beer from breweries across the globe.

69___The Memorial for The French School

When the bombs landed in the wrong place

A nun shields two children who are looking up at the sky; perhaps they can hear the planes flying over the city. The figures from 1953 constitute a simple memorial for the Institut Jeanne d'Arc – The French School. It's there to remind us of 21 March, 1945, when the school was bombed by the British RAF.

It was still dark when 18 fighters and two RAF film production units set of from a base in eastern England. They were carrying 36 bombs, and at only 15 metres above ground (so as to avoid detection by German radar), they few across the North Sea towards Denmark. Their aim was to destroy the extensive archive of the members of the Danish resistance, which was housed in the Shell House – the Gestapo headquarters in Copenhagen. The weather at sea was bad, and wind and sea spray left a layer of salt on the windows of the planes, obstructing the crew's view. Before noon, the first wave of planes approached the city from the south. One of the planes hit a lamppost, was damaged and dropped its bombs on an apartment building in Vesterbro, before crashing in a car park on Frederiksberg Allé. The five remaining planes continued on and bombed the Shell House. The mission was a success. A second wave arrived from the west about three minutes later. Their trajectory meant that the pilots saw the smoke from the crashed plane on Frederiksberg Allé before they saw the smoke from the Shell House. The impaired visibility didn't help their navigation, and the planes bombed The French School across from the car park where the first plane had crashed. A third wave of planes came and dropped more bombs on the school, which was soon in ruins, much like the Shell House.

250 people died as a result of the bombing: 60 of them were Nazis at the Shell House, but the 86 children and 18 adults at The French School made up most of the casualties.

JEANNE D'ARC SKOLEN
21. MARTS 1945

Address Frederiksberg Allé 74, 1820 Frederiksberg C | **Getting there** Metro M3 to Frederiksberg Allé; bus 18, 26, 71, 72 to Frederiksberg Runddel | **Tip** In nearby Madvigs Allé is a bunker from the Cold War. The Frederiksberg Archives occasionally open it in the summer and show a 17-minute film about the bombing of the school, featuring the original recordings made by the two British film production units. See stadsarkivet.frederiksberg.dk for more information.

70__The Metropol Building

International art nouveau on Strøget

Most Copenhageners avoid Strøget like the plague, and are happy to leave it to tourists and school groups from other parts of the country. For the right reasons, however, even they might be willing to brave the hoards of people window shopping and pausing abruptly – and if you're there, you might as well go down to the 'cheap' end between City Hall Square and Amagertorv. It's well worth your while.

On Frederiksberggade 16 (part of Strøget), you'll find the Metropol Building, which is one of the few examples of international art nouveau in Copenhagen – odd, really, since so many other European capitals are fairly brimming with buildings in this style.

The architects of the art nouveau movement wanted to create a new style that was detached from past architecture. Their style was full of contrasts – notice for instance how the massive pillars stand in contrast to the large windows and arches. They also drew inspiration from nature, using motifs such as flowers, plants and insects in fanciful interpretations.

The Metropol Building is from 1907 and was designed by Anton Rosen (who also designed Løvenborg – see ch. 65). The striking art nouveau ornaments set it apart from the surrounding buildings, and the richly decorated dome at the top is particularly worth studying – it's a fine example of the detailed, naturalistic ornamentation that characterises the style.

From 1923 to 1980, the building was home to a cinema with the name Metropol, which is still displayed in golden letters at the upper part of the façade. Today it houses a clothing store. Although it was originally intended to be used for shops and other commercial ventures, as is apparent from the large windows, the gigantic signs that are plastered on the columns by the entrance do detract somewhat from the splendour of the building. Nevertheless, it remains spectacular, and a nice reminder of a time when even the most commercial enterprises were beautifully packaged.

Address Frederiksberggade 16 (Strøget), 1459 Copenhagen K | Getting there Bus 2A, 5C, 250S, 10, 23, 33 or Metro M3 to Rådhuspladsen | Tip The cinema Metropol used to be situated in Mikkel Bryggers Gade 8, where the Grand Theatre is now. The Grand Theatre shows art films and independent films and is one of the most popular cinemas in Copenhagen among those who want to see something other than Hollywood blockbusters.

71 Mountain Dwellings
The only mountain in Copenhagen

In Ørestad, on Amager, you'll find the only mountain in Copenhagen. Don't be put off by the fact that it's only 32 metres high. That just means that you can leave all your climbing gear at home – most people can manage the steps.

The Mountain Dwellings (VM-bjerget) is a combined multistorey car park and residential building. The 650 parking spaces are hidden deep within the mountain, while the peaks are made up of 80 apartments spread over 10 storeys. The building was designed by Bjarke Ingels Group (BIG) and Julien De Smedt Architects. It was unveiled in 2008 and has won numerous awards.

As you get closer, you can't miss it. The façade is covered in pictures of snow-topped peaks, which aren't just for decoration, but also hide the cars within. Inside the building, the space is shaped like a mountain cave, with 16-metre-high ceilings and a constantly low temperature. If you drive through the car park, the numerous hairpin turns might make you feel like you're driving up Alpe d'Huez itself. The neon-coloured walls and ceilings that go from light green to warm red and then sky-blue at the top (near the summit) are a remarkable detail, as are the murals inside the car park, representing Scandinavian wildlife atop mountains of wrecked cars.

If you're an invited guest, you can take the lift, which of course moves diagonally upwards like a ski lift going up a mountainside. The general public will have to make do with the stairs that go up along the side of the mountain. They won't take you all the way to the roof, which is covered in hanging, evergreen and self-watering gardens, but you'll get to the top of the car park – and as you stand here facing north-northeast, you have a fantastic view of Amager, and even Øresund on a clear day.

We'll even go so far as to recommend that you come here early one morning, because you'd be hard pressed to find a better view of the sunrise over the Sound.

Address Ørestad Boulevard 55, 2300 Copenhagen S | Getting there Bus 18, 34, 77 or Metro M1 to Bella Center | Tip The Mountain Dwellings are a part of the VM Houses. The two houses, which are shaped like a V and an M, are on the opposite side of Ørestad Boulevard. Since the Mountain Dwellings slant downwards, the residents of the VM Houses can still enjoy the view of Amager from their windows.

72__The Nærum Railway

With the Mølleåen river as your companion

The trip from end to end only takes 13 minutes, but in that brief time you get to see forest, water and culture through the train windows – which are significantly larger than those on the S-trains, so you can really take in the scenery. The Nærum Railway is beyond a doubt one of the three most delightful railways in the Copenhagen area.

The line was first established in 1990 to serve the blossoming industries along the Mølleåen river, which provided water power for several new factories at the time, making the valley through which it runs a cradle of industry in Denmark. Mølleåen is one of Northern Zealand's most beautiful bodies of water and passes through a number of protected natural areas, and you can see many of them from the train.

You can get on at Jægersborg Station and spend the first couple of stops getting comfortable. As soon as you leave Lyngby, nature takes over as you follow the river. You'll soon forget that you've just passed Lyngby main street and the bustle of this city's shopping centre, which briefly shows itself on the horizon. Now you're in a place where magic happens. You might see a troll or a fairy among the trees, or a tired knight quenching his thirst in the river, while his horse has a well-deserved rest. If you get off at Fuglevad Station, you can walk through the forest to Sorgenfri Palace, which belongs to the Royal Family, so you might even see a real prince or princess.

You could also stay on the train and go to Brede, where you can admire (from the outside) the old clothing factory of Brede Works, or walk from the station to the Open Air Museum. This is run by the National Museum and therefore has free admission. (You can also reach the Open Air Museum from Fuglevad Station.)

If you continue on a few stops, we recommend that you get off at either Ørholm Station or Ravnholm Station and walk along the river. You could also, of course, take the full 13-minute trip to Nærum Station.

Route Jægersborg – Nørgaardsvej – Lyngby Lokal – Fuglevad – Brede – Ørholm – Ravnholm – Nærum | Tip There are several places along the river where you can hire canoes. This is a favoured activity among many Copenhageners and is sure to provide a good time for all.

73_Nature Centre Amager and Kalvebod Commons

Up close and personal with the Ice Age

Borrow a game, says a sign hanging on the hut. Underneath it, you'll find equipment for outdoor games like rounders or capture the flag. You can also rent a stick for cooking the traditional campfire snack of twisted bread, as another sign proudly proclaims. Meanwhile, chickens run past while families grill sausages and a group of people wait impatiently to go butterfly spotting.

This is Nature Centre Amager, a teaching area in the spectacular setting of the Kalvebod Commons. If you want to explore the commons on your own, you can rent bicycles and boxes of exploration gear such as fishing nets or magnifying glasses, or you can borrow a map with suggested trails to follow. The Nature Guides also give tours around the area: there is of course the butterfly spotting tour, but the guides can also teach you about edible plants and mushrooms, local birds and much more. And if you stay at the Nature Centre, you can spin wool or make your own keychain from natural materials.

Kalvebod Commons came about in the late 1930s and early 1940s through state-funded damming, the point of which was to create jobs during the Depression.

When the dam was completed, the 2,500 hectares (or 20 square kilometres) fell into disuse for decades, and flora and fauna were given room to grow and create a unique landscape. The nature in Kalvebod Commons resembles the Northern European tundra as it was just after the end of the last Ice Age, 13,000 years ago.

Since 1990, the whole southern part has been a protected bird reserve, and people aren't allowed there. No fertiliser or pesticides are used, so frogs, toads, salamanders and any manner of insects have supreme living conditions on the commons, and the forest is kept down by allowing cattle, deer, sheep and horses to graze there. They help Copenhagen maintain its Ice Age landscape.

Address Nature Centre Amager, Granatvej 3–15, 2770 Kastrup, www.facebook.com/naturcenteramagere | Getting there Bus 33 to Foldbyvej; Metro M1 to Vestamager | Hours Tue–Fri 9am–3pm, Sat & Sun 10am–4pm (5pm in warmer weather), but check the Facebook page in advance | Tip On Kalvebod Commons you can also visit Pinseskoven, Denmark's largest birch tree forest.

74 _ The Northern Mosaic Cemetery

The secret burial ground

Until 2011, the Northern Mosaic Cemetery was somewhat of a secret wilderness in the otherwise densely populated neighbourhood of Nørrebro. Only Jews were allowed in – with the possible exception of children who accidentally kicked their ball over the stone wall. Over the years, many gentiles asked for permission to enter, and this led to the leaders of the Jewish community suggesting to the City that there could be limited visiting hours. In exchange for opening the site for a few days a week, the City was to pay for the renovation of the cemetery, including clearing out the overgrown bushes and laying paths.

Jewish beliefs prohibit the removal of graves, and there are many headstones which were laid when the cemetery first opened in 1693, when David Israel was the first Jew to be buried in Copenhagen. His headstone can still be seen today. The cemetery was expanded several times throughout the 18th and 19th centuries until 1855, when it reached its current size of 13,500 square metres. At that point, 5,500 people had been buried and there was no room left for new burials, so the Jewish community founded the Western Mosaic Cemetery in 1886. This is located in the southwestern part of Copenhagen.

Many headstones were destroyed over the years, for instance during the English bombing of Copenhagen in 1807, and there are about 2,800 left. The inscriptions show the development of the Jewish community's integration into Danish society, as the oldest feature only Hebrew writing, then a mixture of the two, and the newest have only Danish writing. The social climb undertaken by parts of the Jewish community is also evident in names of the deceased, as many Danes will recognise them as people who founded successful companies, were patrons of the arts or made significant contributions to the financial sector.

Address Møllegade 12, 2200 Copenhagen N (entrance from the corner of Møllegade / Guldbergsgade) | **Getting there** Bus 5C to Kapelvej; bus 1A, 5C, 350S to Elmegade | **Hours** 3 Apr – 30 Sept, Sun – Thu 3 – 7pm. Men are required to cover their heads, so if you haven't brought a hat, you can borrow a yarmulche. | **Tip** The Danish Jewish Museum (see ch. 27) sometimes offers guided tours of the cemetery for smaller groups. See their website jewmus.dk or contact them at info@jewmus.dk for more information.

75__ The Old Village in Valby
Small-town life sprinkled with stardust

Not many of the old villages on the outskirts of Copenhagen remain today, but in the suburb of Valby, around Tingstedet (the former village centre) you can still find some remnants of times past.

Around 30 to 40 years ago the area was in disrepair, but since then the Copenhagen municipal government has – at the request of the area's residents, who didn't want to see it fall completely into ruin – begun a careful restoration of the buildings, as well as building new housing that fits in stylistically with the old washed or painted exteriors.

At Tingstedet (which roughly translates as 'the council place') you'll find the stones that once served as seats for the village council all the way back to the Middle Ages. However, the stones aren't originals, but copies made to recreate the historical surroundings.

You can take a stroll down Mosedalsvej and perhaps go by the new park, a modern version of the old village pond, where villagers would bathe, wash their clothes and fetch water for the house. The water is long gone, but the little park was opened in 2013 where it used to be. On the large façade from Gadekærvej towards the park, author Morten Søndergaard has established a 'gable of dreams' by collecting the dreams and wishes of 117 Valby residents and having them projected unto the house; a lovely sight, especially after dark.

Further down Mosedalsvej, you'll find Nordisk Film, the third-oldest film studio in the world and the oldest still in operation. At weekends, you can take a tour of the studio and see sets and props from some of the studio's most famous productions. Some of the streets surrounding the studio also bear witness to the stars of Danish cinema, such as Asta Nielsen Strædet (named after the greatest Danish silent-film actress and one of the first international film stars) or Erik Ballings Vej (named after the director, who created some of the most beloved Danish films and TV series, such as the series of films about the notorious fictional crime gang Olsen Banden).

Address Tingstedet, Mosedalvej, Smedestræde, Asta Nielsen Strædet, Valby Gadekær, 2500 Valby | Getting there S-train B, Bx, C, H to Valby; bus 26 to Tingstedet | Tip You can take in the small-town atmosphere of Valby and Tingstedet in one of the many cafés and restaurants in the area, such as Café Asta or Café Ciré.

76__Oluf's Ice Cream
Why eat a cone, when there are lollies?

Instagram and Facebook overflow with ice lollies in all the colours of the rainbow, dipped in light or dark chocolate and sprinkled with almonds, nuts or coconut. Following Oluf's Ice Cream often makes for a mouth-watering experience, since they use social media to post pictures of their ice cream of the day.

Fortunately, you don't have to settle for pictures, as all the lollies can be bought in Olufsvej 6 in Østerbro. Their selection is enormous – you can get a liquorice ice cream covered in lemon chocolate or flavours such as mint, raspberry or orange.

The little ice cream shop has long been a favourite among the residents of Østerbro, and the rest of the city now seems to have discovered it as well. The ice cream is Italian, the chocolate is of very high quality, and you can almost taste the love with which each ice lolly is made.

Part of the old-time charm of the shop is the very formal tone with which you're greeted. Denmark is an informal society, and most people would be rather taken aback – if not offended – if you addressed them with the formal 'De' rather than the everyday 'du', perhaps prompting them to ask just how old you think they are! Yet in a little speciality shop like Oluf's Ice Cream it somehow seems all right.

Making lollies rather than the usual scoops of ice cream in cups or cones is a nice touch. It makes for a totally different and more luxurious experience. Just like you can choose how many scoops you'd like elsewhere, you can choose from different sizes here. They also carry a selection of ice cream cakes. You can even have your very own ice cream made – perhaps with berries from your own garden – and have ice cream delivered at your next party.

Remember to enjoy not only your ice cream, but the entire street of Olufsvej where the shop is located. Its pretty little row houses are like a bouquet of colourful flowers, and strolling past them, it feels as if it's always springtime here.

Address Olufsvej 6, 2100 Copenhagen Ø, www.facebook.com/olufsis | **Getting there** Bus 1A, 14 or Metro M3 to Trianglen | **Hours** Mon–Fri 4–8pm, Sat & Sun noon–8pm, they're closed for the autumn and winter months, see their Facebook page for more information | **Tip** If you don't happen to be going past Olufsgade, you can find their ice cream elsewhere in the city. For example at the coffee chain Riccos Kaffebar, which has branches all over Copenhagen.

77__Øregaard Museum

The shipping magnates' estate with paintings
of Copenhagen

Øregaard Museum can be found in a 200-year-old country estate and is a museum of wealthy Copenhageners and their art. It traces its roots back to the early 19th century, when wealthy Copenhageners would move to the country in summer to get away from the cramped and smelly city.

Øregaard is well worth a visit and so is the surrounding area. Here, you'll find a substantial number of large houses, all of them roughly 100 years old, and now owned by embassies. They're a result of the parcelling-out of these large country estates in the early 20th century in order to build smaller houses. The estate that now houses Øregaard Museum was not divided up because its last owner, the Widow Ohlsen, sold it to Gentofte Municipality in 1917 on the condition that the house and park would be conserved for posterity. Øregaard and its park were designed by the well-recognized French architect and landscape gardener, Joseph-Jacques Ramée (1764–1842), whose buildings and gardens can be found not only in France but also in Germany and the United States. For a long time, the estate was owned by wealthy shipping magnates, perhaps because there was an unobstructed view of the ocean. There still is, even though Mrs Ohlsen's husband sold of a large part off the estate overlooking the sea. Fortunately, he didn't part with the wide Hambros Allé, so he still kept his view.

The museum was a fairly quiet place for many years, until it underwent major refurbishment in 2008, when room was made for a café and special exhibitions. During that time, they also acquired many new paintings by Jens Juel, J. T. Lundbye and Paul Fischer, who painted scenes of central Copenhagen around the turn of the last century. The museum has the largest collection of Fischer's work in the country, so if you're keen to see what famous Copenhagen locations once looked like, this is the place for you.

Address Ørehøj Allé 2, 2900 Hellerup, www.oregaard.dk | Getting there Bus 23, 171, 172 to A. N. Hansens Allé | Hours Wed–Fri 1–4pm, Sat & Sun noon–4pm | Tip Just south of the museum is Gentofte public library (Ahlmanns Allé 6), designed by Henning Larsen Architects and decorated by Per Kirkeby.

78__P. Hertz
Luxury jewellers

It looks solid, the jeweller's that's been here since 1841. That's partly due to the façade, which is covered in larvikite, a Norwegian igneous rock which, like the teak interiors, is from when the shop was refurbished in 1906. This was, incidentally, the same year that Kjær & Sommerfeldt (see ch. 60) became purveyors to the court. This company is also known for luxury items, both of their own making and from famous jewellers like Georg Jensen or newer brands like Emquies-Holstein, who have also worked for Tiffany & Co., Ralph Lauren and Royal Copenhagen.

P. Hertz designs and produces two or three collections a year, some of which become part of their permanent collection. This includes the Harlequin line, featuring 14-karat gold jewel-encrusted bracelets for a mere 58,500 DKK, or the Bubbles line, featuring 14-karat gold earrings for just 3,500 DKK. Repairing and altering older jewellery also makes up quite a large part of their business.

P. Hertz is Copenhagen's oldest jeweller still in operation. It was founded by Peter Hertz (1811–1885), who, upon completing his apprenticeship, travelled around Europe to continue his training. Back home in Copenhagen, he was approved as a master goldsmith in 1834 and opened his own shop in 1841 on the corner of Kronprinsensgade and Købmagergade, which even in those days was one of the busiest streets in Copenhagen. At that time, there was a difference between being a goldsmith and a silversmith: the goldsmith would mainly make jewellery in gold or silver by casting, forging or wire drawing the metals, while the silversmith would make cutlery, cups and pitchers by casting or hammering. Today, the two share a common education.

Until 2007, P. Hertz was run by the fifth generation of the Hertz family, goldsmith Flemming Hertz. When none of his children wanted to run the shop, his daughter-in-law, Berit Hertz, took over. She guarantees that you'll get the same impeccable service regardless of how much you spend.

Address Købmagergade 34, 1150 Copenhagen K, www.phertz.dk | Getting there Bus 2A, 23, 32, 37 or Metro M3 to Gammel Strand; bus 23 or Metro M1, M2, M3 to Kongens Nytorv | Hours Mon–Fri 10am–6pm, Sat 10am–3.30pm | Tip In 1835, Niels Brock Perch opened his tea shop in Kronprinsensgade 5. On Saturdays, there's usually a queue out of the door, and if you wish to visit Perch's Tea Room above the shop, we recommend that you book a table by contacting tearoom@perchs.dk.

79_Paludan Books & Café

The smell of old books and fresh coffee

You could be in Paris, Berlin or London; the smell of freshly brewed coffee and old books is universal, and the whole atmosphere at Paludan is at the same time international and very Danish.

The bookshop – just a stone's throw from the old university buildings – was a student favourite for 50 years, during which the students at the University of Copenhagen would buy their course books upstairs or browse the second-hand novels in the basement. In the 1990s, sales had declined, and as one of the first bookshops in Denmark, Paludan tried adding coffee to the equation around the turn of the millennium.

It was a resounding success, and Paludan is now just as much a café as it is a second-hand bookshop – not just for students any more, but for people from all walks of life. The coffee has been supplemented with a large food menu, so you can enjoy breakfast, brunch, lunch and dinner in this world of books. The food is nothing special, but it's decent and the selection is large, so you can find all the staple dishes of a well-stocked standard café.

The real reason to visit Paludan, however, is the atmosphere. The long history of the place shines through in the beautiful old architectural details, and at the same time it's lively and well-visited, with an interesting library-like feel that sets it apart from any other café. It's still frequented by students, who sit in study groups engaged in deep discussions over their course books, but it's also a meeting place for friends, families, tourists and employees of the university. You might even meet a budding author, slaving away over an unfinished manuscript.

Publishers – both big and small – supply Paludan with their newest offerings, and other books can be ordered specially, but Paludan is mainly a second-hand bookshop these days. They do, however, focus on limited releases such as poetry, philosophy and debate books, which can't be found in mainstream chain bookstores.

Address Fiolstræde 10–12, 1117 Copenhagen K, www.paludan-café.dk | Getting there Bus 5C, 6A, 150S, 14, 184, 185; Metro M1, M2 or S-train A, B, Bx, C, E, H to Nørreport | Hours Café: Mon–Thu 9am–10pm, Fri 9am–11pm, Sat 10am–11pm, Sun 10am–10pm; bookshop: Mon–Fri 10am–6pm, Sat 10am–3pm | Tip Paludan isn't the only bookshop with a café in Fiolstræde. Why not pop in to the French Book Café at number 16 and practise your French?

80__Park Bio

A neoclassical trip to the pictures

Ready to go to the cinema? Splendid. Did you remember your glasses? Oh, you didn't? Just as well we're going to Park Bio, which keeps glasses on hand to lend to its more forgetful patrons. That is just one of the services provided by this friendly neighbourhood cinema.

The cinema does not look like much from the outside, but as soon as you walk through the entrance of Østerbrogade, you're met by a wide marble staircase with a brass bannister and replicas of statues from a time gone by. The stairs lead up to a ticket office and snack bar in the foyer, which despite its size feels like a friendly – albeit somewhat kitschy – living room. There are sofas to relax in, crayons and paper on the tables for the children to use, and the room is decorated with statues great and small, palm trees, an aquarium, mirrors and all sorts of knick-knacks. Light comes in from the dome in the roof, which allows the sun to peep in. It's a nice place to be, and you may immediately get the urge to buy a cup of coffee, perhaps forget about the film and just get comfortable in a sofa instead.

Park Bio is the only cinema in Østerbro. It was once called the Park Theatre and took up all of the building, with a vestibule and screening room in what is now a supermarket. The cinema closed down in the 1970s and the first floor (formerly the gallery of the old theatre) reopened as Park Bio. The neoclassicist building was built in 1926 and designed by Arthur Wittmaack and Vilhelm Hvalsøe, who also designed the adjacent Øbro public pool and Østerbro stadium in the same style.

Park Bio doesn't limit itself to normal viewings of the standard Hollywood productions and family-friendly Danish flicks. It also hosts special viewings for the elderly and for nursing mothers, and once in a while it live-streams opera performances from some of the world's largest opera houses. It's even possible to rent an entire viewing room for a private event.

Address Østerbrogade 79, 2100 Copenhagen Ø, www.park-bio.dk | Getting there Bus 1A to Gustav Adolfs Gade; bus 1A, 14 or Metro M3 to Trianglen | Tip Have a cup of coffee on Gunner Nu Hansen's Square nearby, where you can admire the public pool and the stadium.

81 __ The Paternoster Lift
Round and round it goes

In the entrance hall of the castle-like building on Vognmagergade 8 is an old-fashioned paternoster lift. Up and down it goes, all through the day, and it's been doing so since 1913, when the building was erected. A sign admonishes: *When ascending dismount at the latest on the 4th floor; when descending dismount at ground level at the latest.* Below this, however, is a statement that there is no danger connected to staying in the lift when it travels above the top and below the ground floor, so by all means try that if you're feeling brave. The paternoster lift is a sort of cyclical or looped elevator, consisting of a chain of open compartments. The most likely explanation for the name, which means 'Our Father', is that the loop can be compared to the rosary used by Catholics to count their prayers.

There are only five paternoster lifts left in Copenhagen today. The best-known one can be found at Christiansborg, the seat of the Danish Parliament, but to the great disappointment of school children on field trips, it's off-limits to visitors. Not so this one, which is in frequent use by students at the secondary education school of KVUC, who moved into the building in 2007.

The imposing building was originally erected for the Copenhagen gas and electricity services, and above the main entrance it still bears the granite letters signifying its function as home to the *illumination service offices*. The design of the entrance gate, with its bombastic shapes and the three towers of the Copenhagen coat of arms, is reminiscent of the Secession style, the Austrian version of art nouveau. The characteristics of this style can be seen in the interiors, too, for example in details such as the ram's horns on the double doors. Most of the house, however, is built in the Danish National Romantic style with hand-moulded bricks and half-timbered gables. It is as if the two architects, Gustav Hagen (1873–1941) and Rolf Schroeder (1872–1948), each got to leave their mark on the building.

Address Vognmagergade 8, 1120 Copenhagen K, www.kvuc.dk | Getting there Bus 5C, 6A, 150S, 14, 184, 185; Metro M1, M2 or S-train A, B, Bx, C, E, H to Nørreport | Hours Mon–Thu 7am–10pm, Fri 7am–6pm | Tip There are two other paternosters which can be used by the public. One is in the city hall of Frederiksberg, on Smallegade 3 (Mon & Thu 9am–5pm, Tue, Wed & Fri 9am–1pm), and on Axeltorv 3 (Mon–Fri 9am–5pm).

82 The Playground on Hauser Square

Welcome to the land of the Teletubbies

Asphalt, an underground car park and a small, traditional playground covered in graffiti and perhaps some greenery. Those were the main elements of Hauser Square (Hauser Plads) a few years ago, when it was one of the top five most boring playgrounds in Copenhagen. All this changed in the early 2010s, when the City gave it a much-needed makeover as they were building new municipal offices in the area anyway.

An architectural competition was announced in 2008 and won by the Danish Polyform Architects and the Dutch karres+brands, who agreed that they didn't want to fill up the square with dull office buildings. Instead, they looked down and decided to turn the old car park into offices. Although the offices are below ground, the amoeba-shaped openings allow for light to shine in and doubles as a staff courtyard.

On street level, a new and quite unique playground has been built up around the amoeba hole, and it looks like something straight out of *Teletubbies*. You can hear shouting, squeals and happy chatter from the many children climbing, crawling and jumping around on the hills and other gear. Among the more traditional swings and climbing frames are trees, grass, egg shapes and concrete sculptures for the children to 'conquer'. The architecture is deliberately minimalistic and has a very clean and Scandinavian look to it, quite different from the standard idea of a primary-coloured play space.

In true big-city style, parents can let their children play on the enclosed playground while they drink lattes at the nearby café. When the children are tired, you can also take them over to Kultorvet, where there are many cafés. If you'd rather pack your own lunch than pay for one, there's room for that too – a large circular bench right next to the playground.

Address Hauser Plads, 1127 Copenhagen K | **Getting there** Bus 5C, 6A, 150S, 14, 184, 185; Metro M1, M2 or S-train A, B, Bx, C, E, H to Nørreport | **Tip** Visit Restaurant Schønnemann on Hauser Plads. They have been serving classic Danish food, such as herring and open-faced sandwiches (called smørrebrød) since 1877. And, of course, no meal is complete without a schnapps!

83 Pyckler's Bastion

The assault on Copenhagen in 1659

Most Danes remember the stories about the many wars Denmark has fought against Sweden, especially as part of the Northern War of 1657–1660, and not least the Assault on Copenhagen on 11 February, 1659, when the citizens of Copenhagen helped King Frederik III defeat the Swedes at Christiansborg, Christianshavn and Vesterport (what is now City Hall Square). Few people know, however, that the Swedes also attacked at Nørreport and Østerport (once the city gates, now train stations). The attack on Østerport took place in what is now the Østre Anlæg park.

The Swedish King Carl X Gustav had invaded much of Denmark by fighting his way up through Jutland. In early 1658, his army crossed the frozen straits, and Funen, Zealand and the islands to the south were under Swedish dominion. This lead to the Treaty of Roskilde in February 1658, where Denmark brokered peace by handing the areas Scannia, Halland and Blekinge over to the Swedes (and they remain Swedish today).

This wasn't enough for Carl Gustav, however, and in August 1658 he returned to Zealand, this time to capture Copenhagen, and with it, dominion over the whole kingdom of Denmark-Norway.

The Battle of Østerport was dramatic and bloody, but today it's mainly remembered in the name of the remaining bastion, named after the Dutch commander Eustachius Pyckler.

In the early morning of 11 February – while the assault on Christiansborg raged on – Pyckler spotted a Swedish battalion sneaking up on him. He ordered his forces to stay calm until the Swedes had crossed the moat. Then he gave the order to open fire, and a massacre ensued. The Danish and Dutch troops easily picked off the advancing Swedes one by one. The Swedes abandoned the attack at 7am, at which point they had 500 dead and 898 wounded. Only 12 Danes died.

Both the bastion and redoubt (a ravelin) are well preserved.

Address Østre Anlæg, 2100 Copenhagen Ø | Getting there Bus 6A, 150S, 14, 184, 185 to Sølvtorvet; bus 23, 27; Metro M 3 or S-train A, B, Bx, C, E, H to Østerport | Tip In the Swedish Church (Folke Bernadottes Allé 4, by Østerport Station), there is a memorial plaque for the fallen Swedish soldiers.

84__Queen Louise's Bridge

A touch of Paris in a uniquely Danish way

The opulent bridge is somewhat of a paradoxical crossing from the centre of Copenhagen to the densely populated former working-class neighbourhood of Nørrebro. It's named after the wife of Christian IX, who bore him six children, including three who became the Queen Consort of England, the King of Greece and the Empress Consort of Russia. The bridge's impressive pedigree doesn't discourage the many graffiti artists who descend upon the sides of the bridge when the lakes freeze over. Nor does it deter the groups of youths who have adopted the wide pavements as their hangout since 2011. The pavements were laid down when Nørrebrogade was converted into bus and bicycle lanes, and a number of benches were installed on the sunny side of the bridge.

The first bridge in this place was a 16th-century wooden structure, and in the 17th century, a combined dam and bridge was put in place. The current bridge, which was opened in 1887 on the 70th birthday of Queen Louise, was designed by Vilhelm Dahlerup, who also drew a number of other historicist buildings, such as the Royal Theatre and the Lake Pavilion situated between Peblinge Lake and St Jørgen's Lake. A lot of granite was used for the bridge, and it's framed with four flagpole-bearing pedestals, each of which is decorated with a bellicose variation of Copenhagen's coat of arms. The design is heavily inspired by the Empire style of Paris, which was the model for all 19th-century metropolises.

On sunny days, the bridge will be teeming with people. Blankets are spread out on the pavements and there are usually several – very large – ghetto blasters playing music. When there's no more room on the bridge itself, the four plots of grass at each corner of the bridge will also be used. After dark, you can experience a large display of neon signs, on top of the buildings on the Nørrebro side of the bridge, including the hen from the supermarket Irma, who has 'lived' there since 1953.

Address Dronning Louises Bro, 2200 Copenhagen N | Getting there Bus 5C to Søtorvet; bus 5C, 14 to Nørre Farimagsgade | Tip The lakes have a combined circumference of 6.35 kilometres, if you feel like walking – or running – around them.

85 __ Refshaleøen

A smorgasbord of experiences

Refshaleøen offers a long list of activities and experiences. It's one of the few places that has not yet been subject to the City's desire to redevelop and build commercial and residential buildings for Copenhagen's middle class. It probably will be soon, but so far the artificial island remains a melting pot of recreation and creativity.

The man-made island was established in 1868 and has been home to various industrial buildings, including the large Burmeister & Wain Shipyard until its bankruptcy in 1996. Some factories remain, but they take up little room on the large island, where nature goes hand in hand with the numerous activities and family houseboats that have found their place here – along with start-up offices, creative labs and artist's and recording studios, among them that of legendary Danish rock band D-A-D.

You can try your hand at wakeboarding, paintball, climbing, skateboarding, bungee jumping and BMX biking, let out your inner culture vulture in the Copenhagen Contemporary art gallery, or go hunting for a bargain at the flea markets. Should you get hungry while you're here, they've got you covered. You could go to Halvandet, which was the place to eat a few years back and is still open for business, although it's slightly easier to get a table now. Most of the year you can also visit Refen, a large street-food market with a focus on sustainability and start-up culture, and with creative workshops mixed in among the food stalls.

Refshaleøen is also the venue for a number of events and festivals throughout the year. This is where the heavy metal festival Copenhell takes place each summer, and where the final party of Copenhagen Distortion – a celebration of 'street life and new dance music' is held (mercifully removed from the rest of the city).

The island is perfect for exploring on foot or by bicycle, and you can enjoy its twists and turns as well as the nature and the sea. There's absolutely no reason to come here by car!

Address Refshaleøen, 1433 Copenhagen K, www.refshaleoen.dk | Getting there Bus 2A
to Refshaleøen | Tip Each year in June, Refshaleøen hosts the Copenhell Festival, which
focuses on death metal and black metal. If you're a headbanger, then this is the place for you!

86 The Rose Garden

A piece of the 17th century in Frederiksberg

It's not altogether easy to find the public playground and modest park called the Rose Garden. It's surrounded by houses and the only entrances are on the residential cul-de-sac Hortensiavej, or off a narrow path by the small houses on Allégade. However, passing those houses gives you a feel for how Frederiksberg looked in the 17th century. At that time, Allégade was the main street in the Ny Hollænderby (New Dutch Town), and all around it were farms with gardens. The gardens are still here, but the farms are long gone. The new farmers came from the Dutch community which had sprung up in Amager in the 16th century, and they tended to the royal farmlands, which made up all of what is the Municipality of Frederiksberg today. Throughout the 16th and 17th centuries, rich Copenhageners bought up the farms and turned them into summer residences. Only one of these remains today, Ludvigsminde at Allégade 22, which was built around 1770 (have a look inside the courtyard).

The path between the small houses is just wide enough for a tram to pass through, because where the Rose Garden is now was once the Allégade tram depot. It was used by nine tramlines and was closed down in 1966, when the municipality bought the land. They planned for many years to use the depot as a community centre or sports area, as had been done in many other places in Copenhagen. It was torn down in 1975, however, and two years later the area became the Rose Garden.

The park isn't among the most popular in Frederiksberg, but it has a faithful following, including parents either dropping off or collecting their children from the nursery nearby. A little further down Hortensiavej is Edison, part of the Betty Nansen Theatre, which seats 300 people. The building is from 1899 and was built for the Hortensia Plant, which supplied electricity to the first electric trams in Denmark – the same trams that would use the depot which is now a playground.

Address Allégade 20A-20B, 2000 Frederiksberg | Getting there Bus 9A, 18, 31, 71, 72, 74 to Frederiksberg Rådhus; bus 18, 26, 71, 72 to Frederiksberg Runddel; Metro M3 to Frederiksberg Allé | Tip There are some restaurants and cafés with outdoor seating in Allégade, just like in the 19th century, when Copenhageners would go for picnics in what was then rural Frederiksberg.

87 — Rosenvænget
How the other half lives

Fourteen million DKK. That's what an apartment in the Rosenvænget area would set you back. Admittedly that would buy you 600 metres square to roam around, but it's still fairly unattainable for most of us.

Rosenvænget is for the well-off. That's how it's always been. Ordinary people with ordinary salaries will just have to settle for walking up and down the streets, peeking jealously over the hedges at the big, beautiful houses – which is worth doing, we might add, because they're quite something.

It's hard to say when it's best to come by. Maybe in the spring when the trees blossom, the sun shines from a blue sky and the birds tweet merrily. Or in the summer when the hollyhocks are in full bloom of pinks and purples, the barbecues are lit and you can almost smell the chilled white wine being poured. Autumn has its charms as well, however, as you watch the leaves fall in radiant colours, the wind catches your hair and you can meet the residents raking the pavements in front of their houses. Or perhaps a winter's evening, one where the snow has just fallen and the moon lights up your white footprints. It's hard to imagine the weather ever being bad in Rosenvænget.

Denmark's oldest neighbourhood of detached houses was created between 1857 and 1873, when wine merchant Mozart Waagepetersen (1813–1885) parcelled out the land. A fence with a locked gate was put up on the main street, Rosenvængets Hovedvej, leading out to Strandpromenaden, in order to keep out the hoi polloi. This was a nice, calm and proper neighbourhood, and through encumbrances for the area, Waagepetersen decreed that houses should be no more than three storeys high. This has meant that Rosenvænget has remained a neighbourhood of detached houses in the middle of the big city, although some high-rises have sneaked in at the edge of the neighbourhood. Even ordinary people might be able to afford to live in them, as the cheapest apartments cost two million DKK. That will only get you about 50 metres square, but at least you'll be able say you live in Rosenvænget.

Address Rosenvængets Allé, Rosenvængets Sideallé, Rosenvængets Hovedvej, A. F. Kriegers Vej (formerly Rosenvængets Tværvej), 2100 Copenhagen Ø | Getting there Bus 14 to Hobrogade; bus 1A, 14 or Metro M3 to Trianglen | Tip The first residents of Rosenvænget were manufacturers, officers, merchants and master craftsmen, who used their houses as summer residences. There were also celebrities of their time, such as composer J. P. E. Hartmann, politician A. F. Krieger, painter Wilhelm Marstrand and last but not least actress Johanne Luise Heiberg. The great Mrs Heiberg lived at Rosenvængets Hovedvej 46.

88_ SEB Bank and The City Dune

When architecture adjusts for global warming

A walk down Kalvebod Brygge isn't necessarily the most exciting experience. The rather dull commercial properties that were put up in the 1990s block the view of the harbour, and the traffic from the ring road is busy and noisy. All that changes, however, when you reach the corner of Bernstorfsgade and the Swedish bank, SEB's Danish headquarters.

The two 10-storey buildings with soft corners and curves, large expanses of glass combined with green colours and copper coating are more like sculptures, and are among the city's most beautiful buildings from recent years, adding some much-needed lustre to Kalvebod Brygge.

The buildings were created by Lundgaard & Tranberg Architects, who have certainly left their mark on modern Copenhagen (see ch. 50). Surrounding the towers are offices and common areas facing the street and the daylight, while the stairs, restrooms and elevators are located towards the middle of the building.

The two SEB houses are tied together by the City Dune, created on top of a car park by urban space consultants SLA. The Dune consists of white folded concrete with rich vegetation that rises seven metres in the air. It begs to be visited, and fortunately that's exactly why it's there. Via steps and hairpin bends, the Dune twists and turns upwards. Trees, grass and moss make it feel like a lush maze, and the short walk sparks your imagination, and your mind wanders to the Swedish mountains.

The City Dune isn't all fun and games, however; under the landscape are water tanks that collect rainwater and send it back into the atmosphere as humid air. This solution was chosen because the Nordic countries are moving towards a warmer and wetter climate, with more torrential downpours to follow.

Address Bernstorffsgade 50, 1577 Copenhagen V | Getting there Bus 5C, 7A, 26, 68 to Polititorvet | Tip From the top of the City Dune, you can walk directly onto the roof garden of the National Archives and from there onto the roof of Tivoli Hotel. There is a fine view of the railway tracks between Dybbølsbro Station and Copenhagen Central Station, with Vesterbro in the background.

89__The Shooting Range Gardens

From shooting ground to playground

'You've shot the parrot there' is one of many strange Danish animal-related sayings (others involving 'a cow on the ice' or 'owls in the bog' are particularly odd). Most Danes use it when commenting on someone's good fortune, but few are likely to know that the saying derives from private societies like the Royal Copenhagen Shooting Society, which used to meet here in the Shooting Range Gardens (Skydebanehaven), and traces its roots all the way back to the Middle Ages. It still exists, but is no longer in Vesterbro, where they had a clubhouse built in the 1780s.

The ground now belongs to the City, and the house was for a time the Museum of Copenhagen while the gardens were made into a park and playground, where there are lots of things to do for children of all ages and the paddling pool is open in the summer. It's aimed at small children, but everyone is welcome.

The playground is known as the Parrot Playground, and the large wooden parrot is meant to be the landmark of the area, which was last renovated in 2010. However, most people think of the wall (made to look like a medieval wall) as its landmark instead. Built in 1887, the gate was where the Shooting Society would try to shoot the actual parrot – or at least a parrot-shaped target. It was made of wood covered with iron fittings, which were to be shot off in a certain order. There were prizes along the way, and whoever shot the chest plate off would be crowned 'bird king'. This could take up to four or five hours, so there was time for socialising and other competitions along the way. The biggest celebration was the annual Royal Bird Shooting, attended by the king. A long line of Danish kings have been members of the Shooting Society, and it was a sign of prestige to be the king's 'shooting brother' – and certainly not harmful to your career.

Address Absalonsgade 12, 1658 Copenhagen V. There are also entrances off Istedgade 68–80 and Eskildsgade 10–12. | **Getting there** Bus 7A to Vesterbros Torv; bus 23 to Saxogade; Metro M3 to Enghave Plads | **Hours** The playground is manned Mon–Fri 9am–5pm (in summer to 6pm & Sat 10am–5pm), but the area is always open | **Tip** Istedgade might well have the biggest contrasts of any street in the city: there are prostitutes, drug addicts, homeless people and dreary bars at the end closest to the Central Station, and wine bars, fancy restaurants and designer shops at the other.

90__The Sjællandsgade Baths

Fancy going to the sauna?

There's a fairly famous episode of the series *Friends*, where Monica teaches Chandler to take a proper bath. One of those baths where the tub is full of sweet-smelling bubbles and the steam rises from the hot water, you have a glass of champagne in your hand and a towel on which to rest your head. That's almost what you get in Sjællandsgade, where you can pay to take a bath. Or perhaps you'd like to go to a sauna without all the hassle of going to a public pool? Look no further!

The Sjællandsgade Baths are somewhat of an anachronism; a public bathhouse established in 1917, which is still up and running 100 years later, even though all the old working-class housing has been modernised. You might think there's no need for a public bath, and that was exactly the assumption the City made when they closed it down in 2010.

In fact, there are more than 23,000 apartments without private showers in the Municipality of Copenhagen, and close to 4,000 in Frederiksberg (many buildings have communal showers in the basement or attic). This is why the employees of the Sjællandsgade Baths and other locals banded together to form an organisation that would preserve the baths. They maintain that a bathhouse provides more than just a place to bathe – it's a place to discuss health and culture and to make new friends.

The City pays the rent and utilities for the baths, but they're run by volunteers. The building is listed and has been totally renovated so that it meets modern standards, and the volunteers engage in local causes such as sustainability, integration and encouraging healthy lifestyles. Their mission is to create a place that – like the bathhouses of ancient Rome – is an integral part of the cultural and health-related life in the area. To do this, they work closely with the Metropolitan University College nearby, where students of health or nutrition help disadvantaged and at-risk residents.

Address Sjællandsgade 12A, 2200 Copenhagen N, www.sjaellandsgadebad.dk/en_GB | Getting there Bus 5C to Sjællandsgade | Hours Tue 3–9pm, Wed 3–8pm (8–9pm, aromatherapeutic sauna), Fri 4–8pm (men and women can bathe together), Sat 9am–3pm, Sun noon–1pm (aromatherapeutic sauna) | Tip The Baths are on Guldberg Square (Guldberg Plads), a lovely place to sit and watch people go by. The square is also a public playground and schoolyard for a nearby school.

91__Sluseholmen

A pinch of Amsterdam with a sprinkling of jazz

Canals have replaced pathways and streets on Sluseholmen, and there aren't many places in Copenhagen where the residents have pontoons and kayaks instead of balconies and gardens.

If you feel like you've taken a wrong turn and wound up in Amsterdam while walking around the area, the eight little islets that constitute Sluseholmen have served their purpose. The development is based on the trendy Amsterdam neighbourhoods Java Island and Borneo Island, and in fact all three areas share an architect – the Dutchman Sjoerd Soeters.

At the same time, the numerous blocks reflect the history of Copenhagen, and you can find similar blocks from the 17th and 18th centuries in Christianshavn and around Amalienborg Palace, respectively.

In order to create variation in the buildings, 25 different architects' studios were employed. Each block has had at least five studios working on it and they vary in height – between four and seven storeys – all in order to ensure diversity. To avoid Sluseholmen becoming a sleepy or even dead area (as is unfortunately seen in some of the other newer neighbourhoods in Copenhagen), supermarkets, cafés and nurseries were built on the ground floors from the very beginning.

The streets on Sluseholmen are named after American jazz musicians who settled and played in Copenhagen between the 1960s and 1980s.

Sluseholmen is an artificial island created in the 1940s for industrial purposes. Large Danish companies such as Aalborg Portland and shipping company DFDS had facilities here. As the south harbour became less utilised as a port during the 1980s and 1990s, the companies disappeared gradually as well. In the late 1990s, the City and Copenhagen Harbour opened up the area for development, and the first residents arrived in 2006.

Address Sluseholmen, 2450 Copenhagen SV | Getting there Bus 7A to Thad Jones Vej/
Ernie Wilkins Vej | Tip Stroll across the Teglværksbroen Bridge to Teglholmen. There are
many interesting buildings here – both residential and commercial – and it's still possible
to see the remains of the industrial port.

92 Sögreni Bicycle Shop

A bike ride with attention to detail and material

What do you get the cyclist who has everything? The Sögreni Bicycle Shop in Sankt Peders Stræde can help with that. How about a designer bell made of brass, steel, copper or zinc? Or perhaps a stylish front carrier in aluminium and marine plywood? In general, Sögreni's bikes and accessories are characterised by special materials, and more unusual ones such as wood or bamboo.

Sögreni is Søren Gregers Nielsen, who has had a workshop in this street since 1980, when he first started making his own bicycle frames. In the late 1990s, he aimed to make the first wooden bike in the world, and was given 100,000 DKK by the Ministry for Culture to help him achieve this goal. Sögreni has long caught the eye of the established design community, which resulted in a collaboration with the Louisiana art museum in the mid-1990s on a bicycle called the Sögreni Classic.

Sögreni didn't pick Sankt Peders Stræde by accident either. This was where the alternative milieu first began to make its mark on the area, which also includes Studiestræde, Larsbjørnsstræde, Larslejsstræde and Teglgårdstræde – collectively known as 'The North Quarter'. Colloquially, it's rather unappealingly called 'the Piss Gutter', a name rooted in the 19th century, when there were many pubs and alcohol manufacturers in the area, the latter of whom kept cattle – so the name is to be taken quite literally. When Sögreni set up shop there were still a few pubs left, and in the neighbouring Larslejsstræde, prostitutes would hang out of the windows while the punters queued up across the street. The neighbourhood was also characterised by small industry which had since moved out to a more modern setting, leaving large spaces available for the alternative milieu to move in.

These days, the alternative feeling has subsided, but there's still a great deal of community spirit in the area, which is most evident in the annual street festivals, where you're welcome to join in.

Address Sankt Peders Stræde 30A, 1453 Copenhagen K, www.sogreni.dk | Getting there Bus 5C to Teglgårdsstræde; bus 2A, 5C, 250S, 10, 23, 33 or Metro M3 to Rådhuspladsen | Hours Mon–Fri 10am–6pm, Sat 10am–4pm | Tip Around the end of Sankt Peders Stræde, where it meets Vester Voldgade, you'll see Jarmer's Tower, the only visible remains of the fortified wall that surrounded Copenhagen in the 14th century. A gate in the fence allows you to get a closer look.

93   Solbjerg Square

A city campus with artificial birdsong

In the evening luminous silhouettes are formed in the coating; during the day, you can run or bike through splashing water and clouds of mist. Some 32 'speaker wells' play birdsong and other sounds, and the Pine Grove is full of students from Copenhagen Business School on their lunch break.

That's what Solbjerg Square (Solbjerg Plads) is like on a good day. It's clean and minimalist, but there's still room for stairs, unexpected planters and self-made trails in what the municipality calls Frederiksberg's New Urban Space.

Urban space consultants SLA have created this green and active space, which is used frequently by pedestrians and cyclists. There are more than 30,000 of them daily, and the metro runs below.

If you come from the direction of Frederiksberg shopping centre, the area stretches out past Frederiksberg secondary school, the public library, courthouse and CBS's main buildings, past Kilen ('the Wedge' – also part of CBS) and out to Andersen's Water Tower from 1877 – ending at Fasanvej Station.

The many interesting buildings haven't quite solved what some reports call the 'backside problem' – not as rude is it sounds, it means that the whole area used to be railway ground, and the surrounding houses therefore faced away from it. There was a railway here from 1864 until 1998, and the old station house is still here – now a café – although it had to be moved to the side in order to make way for the metro.

If the weather isn't good enough for biking or playing outside, there are other options. You could visit Frederiksberg shopping centre or the public library. The latter has one of the country's largest reading rooms in the original part of the library from 1935, and in the new subterranean expansion from 2004, there's a large newspaper reading room with plenty of daylight and a large selection of Danish and foreign newspapers.

Address Solbjerg Plads, 2000 Frederiksberg | Getting there Metro M1, M2, M3 to Frederiksberg; Metro M1, M2 to Fasanvej | Hours Public library: Mon–Thu 10am–7.30pm, Fri 10am–5pm, Sat 10am–3pm, Sun 1–4pm | Tip Kilen ('the Wedge') is officially only open to students and staff, but you'll have no trouble looking inside the large foyer with organically-shaped balconies and a floor that looks like it's been moved here from a Greek island.

94 The Spa at Frederiksberg Public Pool

An old-fashioned pool with a touch of luxury

Ah, breathe it in! Aromatherapy saunas can be found in many places in the city, but here at the spa they're very proud of their sauna masters, who compete internationally and have won both Danish and world championships in a discipline they call 'saunagus' (from the German *Aufguss*, which translates to 'on-pouring'). At the Frederiksberg public pool (Frederiksberg Svømmehal), they offer saunagus hourly on weekdays, but it's incredibly popular, and you can't book a time, so be there early. The spa also offers a whirlpool, various types of showers and another speciality – the salt-water pool, the Dead Sea – where you can float around almost like you're in the real thing.

The spa is a lively place with lots of chatting and laughter, even though it claims to be a silent area, and large groups can book a slot. It's hard to avoid getting close to your fellow bathers, especially on Friday afternoons and Saturdays. Do remember that you're required to wear a swimming costume in the spa.

The Frederiksberg pool, one of the oldest in Copenhagen, is from the 1930s, when the first pools were introduced. It was refurbished at the turn of the millennium, and the spa was added, among other things. In the pool area itself, you'll find the main 25-metre pool with diving boards of varying heights, a heated pool for babies and their parents (subject to booking), a warm-water pool, a pool for kids and a 105-metre-long waterslide.

There is a family area with limited opening hours and water of varying depths. Here, you can admire one of five monumental mosaics created by the artist Vilhelm Lundstrøm for the swimming pool. The mosaics are in the classic modernist style and represent bathers in the nude. If you'd like to see the motif come to life, the association for Danish Naturists arranges nude bathing for any interested parties during the winter, and the spa is packed on these occasions.

Address Helgesvej 29, 2000 Frederiksberg | Getting there Bus 2A or Metro M 3 to Aksel Møllers Have | Hours Mon–Fri 10.30am–8.30pm, Sat, Sun & bank holidays 9.30am–3.30pm; booking must be made in advance at svoemmehal.frederiksberg.dk | Tip The pool is located in a quiet residential area, but is close to two of Frederiksberg's busiest shopping streets with cafés and restaurants – Godthåbsvej and Falkoner Allé.

95 __ The Speedboat Rental at Fisketorvet

Where you go is up to you

Why not sail around Copenhagen Harbour in your own speedboat? You choose the speed, the route and what to see.

The speedboat rental, called Copenhagen Boat Rent, looks more like an allotment garden than anything else, with its little red shed, planters with delicate purple flowers and Danish flag flying. It's quite heart-warming to see that even here, by the Fisketorvet shopping centre and Kalvebod Brygge with its big – often rather ugly – commercial buildings, there's room for something so quaint. Whether the little shed is better looking than the captains of industry is up to you.

You can hire a boat for one, three or six hours, and you only pay for each additional 15 minutes.

You could sail all the way out to the Trekroner Fort (see ch. 106), bring fishing rods and fish by the Slusebroen bridge in Sydhavnen or take a trip out to Nordhavn to see how the building work is progressing in the city's newest neighbourhood. If the weather is in your favour, you can lounge around and enjoy the sunshine in the canals of Christianshavn. There are many opportunities, and as the boat rental's slogan says: where you go is up to you – and the Danish Maritime Authority.

The boats fit five people and none of you need have sailing experience; the 'captain' must, however, be over 18. The good people at the boat rental will show you the ropes.

The speedboat rental isn't the only place in Copenhagen where you can rent a boat. On Islands Brygge 10 you'll find the company GoBoat, another good alternative. The boats you can find here are equipped with a small central table, perfect for balancing a bottle of bubbly and a bowl of fresh strawberries on your cruise through the harbour.

Address Copenhagen Boat Rent, Fisketorvet, 1561 Copenhagen V, www.copenhagenboatrent.dk | Getting there Bus 10 or S-train A, B, Bx, C, E, H to Dybbølsbro | Hours Mon–Fri 11am–8pm, Sat & Sun 10am–8pm (1 May–1 Sept) | Tip You can also sail across the harbour to Nokken, where you'll find pioneer-style allotments, wild nature and pleasant residents.

96__The Spire Playground
The city of spires built for children

You need to be quick if you want to catch the pigeons on the Børsen spire. Perhaps you could challenge your friends to a competition. At the Round Tower, you can see constellations or walk across to the spire on the City Hall. From here, you can slide down before crawling up the Church of Our Saviour, or make sandcastles in the dome of the Marble Church.

In the Spire Playground (Tårnlegepladsen) in Fælledparken Commons, five of the most famous towers and spires in Copenhagen have been shrunk down, so that children can get to know the city by running around among these scale models. There are classic playground elements such as swings, sandbox, climbing frame, slide and ball cage, as well as interactive elements like the pigeon-catching game. There's also a fire pit, where you can gather to toast marshmallows or make campfire bread when you need a break from playing.

Parents can join in the fun or watch from one of the many benches. The playground is manned between April and September by educated staff, who can help get games started.

You could also bring a scooter and a helmet, because there's a special area nearby just for scooters, which can be used by both beginners and intermediates with a need for speed.

The Spire Playground is just one of the play areas in the Fælledparken Commons. There's also the Sensory Garden, which is laid out to be easy and safe to explore for children in wheelchairs or with impaired vision, with various sculptures and features to discover. Here are plants chosen especially for their interesting smells, a wooden maze with wide passages, gently clinking wind chimes and a small canal, and the atmosphere is calm and peaceful.

A third area of interest is the Water Playground, where you can fire water cannons and play in the paddling pool. The water is only turned on from June to August and when the temperature allows it, but that's probably just as well if you're not looking to catch a cold.

Address Fælledparken, Frederik V's Vej, 2100 Copenhagen Ø | Getting there Bus 1A to Irmingersgade | Tip Other open-air playgrounds in Østerbro can be found on Bopa Plads, in Århusgade and in Rosenvængets Allé.

97 __ St Hans' Square
Street art and missiles

From the top of the Mærsk Building (which houses part of the University of Copenhagen), there is a free view of St Hans' Church (Sankt Johannes Kirke) and St Hans' Square (Sankt Hans Torv), where Guldbergsgade, Elmegade and Fælledvej meet. Today, it's the unofficial centre of the hip Nørrebro, and there's a wide selection of cafés, restaurants and specialist shops.

Some might feel that the cafés and their patrons make a little too much noise, while others may think that the art installation *The House that Rains* is rather too overpowering. The installation (created by Jørgen Haugen Sørensen) was put in in connection with a larger restructuring in 1992–1993, where a formerly busy intersection was (re-)turned into a square with new cobblestones, which unwittingly made history.

During the restructuring, the square was the site of what could have been the most fatal clash between police and protesters since the occupation. The occasion was an EU referendum where a narrow majority of 56.8% of Danes voted to ratify the Maastricht Treaty. A large minority opposed the EU so fiercely that a demonstration on the night of the referendum evolved into serious altercations with the police. The construction work on the square meant that there were piles of little cobblestones, just the right size for throwing. They weighed about 2.5kg each, and tonnes of them were thrown at the police (who occasionally threw them back). The events have been captured on film, which shows that the police first fired warning shots into the air and then fired directly at the protestors' legs. The following four years saw a thorough investigation into the events of that night to find out, among other things, whether an order had been given to shoot, or whether the police officers had fired in self-defence. A total of 11 civilians were injured by the shots, some seriously, while 115 others were injured, 24 of them critically.

Address Sankt Hans Torv, 2200 Copenhagen N | **Getting there** Bus 1A to Sankt Hans Torv; bus 1A, 5C, 350S to Elmegade | **Tip** The streets around the square are full of good restaurants including Kiin Kiin on Guldbergsgade 21 and Bæst at number 29. The concert venue and nightclub Rust at number 8 is also worth a visit, and Elmegade has a large number of little shops, restaurants and cafés, including the Laundromat Café at number 15, where you can also wash your clothes.

98 __ St Peter's Church
Danish-German history renewed

Germany is Denmark's largest trading partner, a fact that's often highlighted when teachers lament their students' lack of interest in learning German. On the other hand, German has become somewhat exotic, which can be seen in the names of hip cafés such as Kreuzberg, Märkbar and Gefährlich.

The German language was an integral part of Danish society until 1864, when Denmark lost the German-speaking parts of the realm. If you'd like to revisit the time before that, you can walk around the chapels and cemetery of St Peter's Church (Sankt Petri Kirke), where you'll find a great number of the German people and families who came to influence political and cultural life in Copenhagen.

The church itself is a regular Danish parish church, but it has a large German congregation dating back to 1585. Back then, the little medieval church, which had survived the Reformation, was given to the large German community, many members of which had emigrated to Denmark during the Thirty Years' War (1618–1648). The Danish monarchs have long been of German extraction to some degree, and there was a large number of German-speakers at the court. In the 17th and 18th centuries, these courtiers and civil servants were part of the congregation. There was therefore never a shortage of money to finance the large developments which were undertaken in the church. The large three-winged chapel complex from 1681 and 1739 was particularly expensive, but the rich and powerful members were happy to pay for it – in return, they were honoured with grand funerals and memorial plaques. The large hall gained special status in the 18th century, as you could admire the many plaques and sarcophagi created by some of the leading artists of the time. The fire of 1728, the bombing of Copenhagen in 1807 and a large refurbishment in the 1860s all took their toll on the buildings and interiors, but a large refurbishment project in the 1990s restored the church to its past glory.

Address Sankt Peders Stræde 2, 1453 Copenhagen K, www.sankt-petri.dk | Getting there
Bus 5C, 6A, 150S, 14, 184, 185; Metro M1, M2 or S-train A, B, Bx, C, E, H to Nørreport |
Hours Apr–Sept Wed–Sat 11am–3pm | Tip If you'd like to see the area from above, there
are several options. The nearby Hotel Sankt Petri at Krystalgade 22 has several rooms overlooking the church. Or you can visit the Round Tower where you can get a 360-degree view
of the city.

99 __ Star Radio

While we wait for the new Resistance Museum

A new façade was unveiled at Istedgade 31 in August 2015. There was much ado, with many speeches and representatives of local media, the street was blocked off and hundreds of people turned up. The façade was certainly lovely – bright lilac with the words *Stjerne Radio* ('Star Radio') written in big black and white letters. But really … a street party for a new façade?!

You'll probably notice it straight away as you walk down the street, because it stands out among the other shops and buildings – it's as if it were from another time. And indeed it is, which is why the unveiling was such a big event. The façade was a recreation of the original façade as it looked in 1943 when Star Radio played a significant part in the Danish Resistance.

Behind the large shop windows is a little exhibition, telling the story of the occupation (1940 – 1945) and the resistance towards the Nazis in both words and pictures. Between 1942 and 1944, the radio shop was central to the resistance movement. They transmitted BBC radio out onto the street – which was not illegal as such, but a blatant provocation of the Nazis. In 1943, they began printing the resistance magazine *De Frie Danske* ('The Free Danes'), and the nationalist resistance group Holger Danske (named after a mythical Danish figure, who 'lives' at Kronborg Castle) was founded in the back room.

In 1944, the shop was bombed by the Peter Group, whose aim was to sabotage the resistance groups. The shop was rebuilt, re-bombed and rebuilt again.

Star Radio closed in 1966, and the building was torn down in 1996 to make way for a wall. An organisation took it upon themselves to re-establish the façade, and we recommend spending a few minutes studying the current exhibition, if you're passing that way. It's a good substitute for the new Resistance Museum, which is set to open in late 2018.

Address Istedgade 31, 1650 Copenhagen V | Getting there Bus 23 to Gasværksvej; Bus 2A, 5C, 7A, 250S, 10, 23, 26, 31, 37, 68; Metro M3 or S-train A, B, Bx, C, E, H to København H | Tip In Victoriagade, just off Istedgade, you'll find Mikkeller Bar and Tante T. The former serves beer from the famous Mikkeller microbrewery, and Tante T ('Auntie T') serves tea and cakes from all over the world. Both places are incredibly popular, so prepare to stand at Mikkeller or book a table at Tante T. See mikkeller.dk and tante-t.dk/bord-reservation.

100 _ Superkilen
Street furnishings and activities from around the world

Some residents were sent to Jamaica to find the ultimate sound system for the area, while others went to St Louis in the United States to find the perfect line dance pavilion. Others supplied stories from their holidays (such as table tennis matches on the streets of Barcelona), and a group of youngsters suggested a Thai boxing ring, which they were going to research themselves. These were just a few of the stories and journeys needed to create Superkilen park between Tagensvej and Nørrebrogade in 2012. The project group felt it was essential to muster local ideas and feelings of ownership, partly because they believed that if the locals were involved with the planning, they would take better care of the area.

Practically all nationalities and age groups in the neighbourhood are represented through objects and plants – approximately 100 different kinds from 57 different places around the globe. Some are more obvious than others, such as the sign for the Russian Hotel Moskvich at one end, and a sign for the American DeAngelis Donuts at the other. Others are less conspicuous, such as the British rubbish bins, but each item has a story and adds to the interesting layout of the park, the purpose of which is to celebrate diversity and stand as an example for high-standard urban development. Should you wonder where a particular object comes from – perhaps an uncomfortable bench or an old-fashioned lamp post – there is a legend at each end of the three areas that make up Superkilen: the Red Square by Nørrebrogade, the Black Square in the middle and the Green Area with hills and grass by Tagensvej.

The Red Square has nothing to do with its namesake in Moscow. This one is named after the idea that 'red' means activity, fun and music, so of course the area had to be painted red – as well as various shades of orange and purple. The colours proved hard to maintain, however, and the original surface turned slippery in rainy weather, so today the painted coating has been replaced by colourful tiles.

Address Nørrebrogade 208, 2200 Copenhagen N | Getting there Bus 5C to Nørrebrohallen; bus 5C, 4A, 250S, 350S, 12, Metro M3 or S-train F to Nørrebro | Tip If you go to the reception desk at the nearby Nørrebrohallen, you can book time for a variety of indoor sports, including basketball, climbing and badminton.

101 The Surgical Auditorium
Classicist architecture and gory displays

You may be familiar with the TV series *The Knick*, where surgeon John W. Thackery (played by Clive Owen) leads a theatrical display as he performs surgery while doctors and other interested parties watch. They sit on benches resembling an amphitheatre and a successful performance is met with applause. This is almost how things were done in the Surgical Auditorium (Kirurgisk Auditorium) of the Royal Academy of Surgeons, which from 1787 to 1842 was where budding surgeons were taught, and is now part of the Medical Museion.

However, the auditorium wasn't used for operations on living patients, but rather for demonstrating surgical techniques on cadavers from the nearby King Frederik's Hospital (see ch. 47). The purpose of these displays wasn't so much to amaze as to teach surgery, which at that time wasn't part of the medical degree at the university, but was a continuation of the education of trained barber-surgeons – craftsmen who performed surgery until the late 17th century. This education had a breakthrough in 1736, when barber-surgeon Simon Crüger founded a school for more systematic and professional teaching of anatomy and surgery. After his death, this teaching was continued through the Academy of Surgeons.

Surgeons and doctors were educated separately until 1842, when the two were merged under the Faculty of Medicine. Teaching continued in the auditorium until 1942, and now it's used for lectures and events at the museum.

The building was designed by architect Peter Meyn (1749–1808), who was heavily influenced by the ancient world, and the ceiling of the auditorium is very clearly inspired by the Pantheon in Rome. These lovely surroundings have been left with practically no sign of their former usage, so you'll have to imagine what it was like to sit here for hours on end looking at – and smelling – the dissection of human remains!

Address Medical Museion, Bredgade 62, 1260 Copenhagen K, www.museion.ku.dk | Getting there Metro M3 to Marmorkirken | Hours Tue–Fri 10am–4pm, Sat & Sun noon–4pm; guided tours in English Tue–Fri 2pm & Sun 1.30pm | Tip The museum has an exhibition of body parts used for teaching, along with misshapen foetuses and other ailments, as well as both historical and biomedical exhibitions.

102 Svaneknoppen

The smallest beach and the largest marina

In the northernmost part of the Municipality of Copenhagen, on the border with Gentofte, the Svaneknoppen ('the Swan Bud') shoots out its 130-metre-long boardwalk. On one side is Svanemøllen Beach, which until 2010 was a closed bay with smelly seaweed. These days, there's 4,000 square metres of beach, every inch of it covered with people during the summer. The water is so clean that there are now 14 different types of fish, including sea trout, cod, garfish and sculpin, and if you have a fishing licence you can fish off the north side of Svaneknoppen.

On the other side of the 'bud' is Svanemøllen Harbour, the largest marina in Northern Europe. It is run by three yacht clubs, with 1,100 berths between them. There are no berths specifically for guests, but the owners are usually good at putting up signs by vacant berths, and visitors are also welcome in the yacht club restaurant.

Before the big harbour developments in the 1880s, you could walk all the way along the coast from the harbour promenade Langelinie. This is no longer possible, but a long wooden jetty was built in the 1930s, with berths on one side and the sea on the other. The present facility is from 2008, when the jetty was so ruined by woodworm that it had to be replaced.

On Svaneknoppen itself is the Svanemøllen Bay Winter Bathing Club with its own jetty – and a sauna with a lovely view on the first floor. The club was founded in 2009 and has a very long waiting list, but if you meet someone with a club bracelet, you can ask about special guest days.

Until 2019, the municipality and the state will be building a tunnel under Svaneknoppen, so there's lots of construction going on. The tunnel will send cars under the water instead of through the streets of central Copenhagen, as it will link up with the new neighbourhood in Nordhavn, which also has plans for a series of boardwalks inspired by Svaneknoppen.

Address Svaneknoppen, 2100 Copenhagen Ø | Getting there Bus 1A, 12, 23 or S-train A, B, Bx, C, E to Svanemøllen | Tip Right by the marina on the first floor of the clubhouse you'll find Café Sundet. It offers decent food and a lovely view of Svanemøllen Bay.

103 — The Theatre Museum
Feel like royalty

Looking for a place to hold your fancy dress party in style? Anyone hosting a large event and wanting a sprinkling of royalty can hire the Theatre Museum.

It was the court theatre at Christiansborg Palace, which became a rococo-style royal residence in 1740, with a chapel and large riding arena surrounded by a symmetrical two-winged building with stables and barns. The theatre was opened slightly later, during the reign of King Christian VII (1749–1808), when the harness storeroom above the stables in one wing was converted into a theatre in 1766. You can still see Christian VII's private box, where he would sit with his queen, Caroline Mathilde, and trusted personal physician, Struensee, who doubled as the queen's lover.

Many grand parties were held in the theatre, including the masquerade balls of the 18th century, where partygoers would wear both costumes and masks. The theatre was therefore built with this in mind, and the floor of the stalls could be raised to the same height as the stage. It was at one of these masquerade balls in the winter of 1772 that Struensee was arrested during a coup d'état, and was later executed in the Eastern Commons, depicted in the 2012 film *A Royal Affair*.

After the coup, no more grand balls were held in the theatre. For a while, it was an annex to the Royal Theatre and housed the ballet academy, where a young Hans Christian Andersen auditioned (unsuccessfully) in 1820.

The Theatre Museum has been housed in the Court Theatre since 1922, and its visitors can go practically anywhere, including on the stage. Unfortunately, you can no longer see the original rococo interiors, but instead the more parlour-like Biedermeier style from 1842. The museum exhibits the history of the theatre from the 18th century to the present day, and if that doesn't do it for you, you can still walk around and feel like royalty.

Address Christiansborg Ridebane 18, 1218 Copenhagen K, www.theatermuseet.dk |
Getting there Bus 2A, 23, 31, 37 to Stormbroen / Nationalmuseet; bus 2A, 23, 32, 37 or
Metro M3 to Gammel Strand | Hours Tue – Thu 11am – 3pm, Sat, Sun & bank holidays
1 – 4pm | Tip The Tower Restaurant at the top of Christiansborg Palace serves traditional
Danish food accompanied by a magnificent view. Reservations at taarnet.dk.

104_ Tippen
It's a bird, it's a plane, it's Tippen

Stoats, bats, lemon butterflies, foxes, pheasants, nightingales and maybe even a tern. That's just a small selection of the wildlife you might encounter if you walk out to Tippen ('the Tip'). It's an impressive list, considering that Tippen is still a fairly 'new' area, which was filled in with construction waste and surplus earth from other parts of town between 1945 and 1973. From then on, the plants and trees were allowed to grow freely, creating an airy natural space, in which many little creatures and birds now thrive.

However, you can also still find traces of the urban waste that makes up the foundation of the entire area, as nature hasn't yet won out everywhere. The first few times you might be surprised when you step directly from soft, green grass and on to asphalt and concrete, but you quickly get used to it – it's simply part of what makes the place unique.

Tippen is neither city, park, nor forest, it's simply Tippen – a wild and free area, which many Copenhageners enjoy visiting all year round. In the spring, they cut blossoming branches for their vases at home, in the autumn they pick apples and berries. There's both water and sky, and there are sheep to help keep the hogweed under control. You'll probably meet them out there, and one of the flocks might keep you company as you stroll around, admiring the landscape.

A nature school was established on Tippen in 2009, and local organisations arrange guided walks around the area focusing on the flora and fauna. There are also volunteers who help keep the area clean and remove some of the more invasive plants that, like the hogweed, threaten to take over the area.

The southern part of Tippen – roughly 32 of the total 52 hectares – is listed. The remaining area is reserved as a recreational space, but people do worry that the City might decide to build housing there. If so, it wouldn't be possible until the 2020s, but many hope that Tippen will be allowed to remain as it is.

Address Sydhavnstippen (Tippen), 2450 Copenhagen SV, www.sydhavnstippen.dk | Getting there Bus 7A, 9A, 18, 23 to Mozarts Plads; bus 9A to Stubmøllevej | Tip You can end your day with a visit to the Children's Animal Farm next to Karens Minde Culture House. There are sheep, chickens, rabbits and horses, which are owned and cared for by children in the area.

105 Træstubben Vesterbro Nature Workshop

From unofficial injection room to children's nature workshop

There is a lone tower at Saxogade 13 that protrudes above something resembling a theatre backdrop. The accompanying church is located in the courtyard, and the tower stands alone, because the houses on both sides have been demolished. This was in connection with a major reorganisation in 1958, when the rear houses were replaced by a green area, the Saxo Park, which extends up to Matthæusgade.

'Park' is perhaps saying too much about this narrow stretch, which quickly gained a bad reputation as an area frequented by drug addicts. The addicts used the park's toilet building as an injection room, so the toilets were closed, and the building stood empty for several years. It was supposed to be demolished, but in 2006, it was lent to a local organisation, who rebuilt it as nature workshop.

Træstubben ('the Tree Stump') works to promote environmental consciousness among the neighbourhood children, working closely with local organisations, nurseries and primary schools. Some of the organisations that support and use the park are the nearby Apostle Church, a scout group and an organisation that distributes surplus food from nearby supermarkets to those in need. All this collaboration means that Træstubben and Saxo Park are well looked after.

It's somewhat difficult to schedule a visit to see what goes on at Træstubben, because things happen spontaneously or informally, and because it's mainly a base for activities that take place all over Vesterbro (such as the Flowering City project, where local residents or groups can adopt a verge). In early May, seeds are handed out in Enghave Park (see ch. 35), and you have to promise to look after your verge. This shouldn't be too difficult, they say, but admit that they face some challenges from cyclists, street parties and scaffolding and lorries – this is a city, after all.

Address Saxogade 17, 1662 Copenhagen V | **Getting there** Bus 7A to Vesterbros Torv; bus 23 to Saxogade | **Tip** Otte Krabbe's Square by Matthæusgade 1 is another example of how to convert an empty development into a park, this one featuring walls, plateaus and benches where the buildings used to be.

106___ Trekroner Fort

See the city from another angle

The area around *The Little Mermaid* is usually packed with tourists from around the world, and the canal boats pass by on the water, allowing people to take pictures. If this isn't your kind of thing, you could take a trip to Trekroner Fort ('Tree Crowns Fortress'), a little island at the entrance to the harbour. You can only sail there from early June to mid-September, but once you're there, you have plenty of opportunities for picnics, parties, conferences or just seeing Copenhagen from another angle.

The island is actually one large fortress and was part of the 18th-century fortifications of Copenhagen, which can still be seen in Christianshavn and Østre Anlæg (see ch. 83). When the Danes fought a large part of the English navy in 1801, the battle was directed from Trekroner, and the fort was also used against the English in 1807. The cannon is from the late 19th century, when the fort became part of a much larger line of fortifications, including the Garderhøj Fort (see ch. 43). During the First World War, there were close to 700 soldiers stationed on the island.

Trekroner was shut down in 1920 along with the rest of the fortifications. It was briefly used to train soldiers to fire cannons, before being used for civilian entertainment, with a cinema, cabaret and dance hall – the kind of place you'd go after hiding your wedding ring in your pocket! During the occupation, the Nazis used it as a barracks and it was outfitted with anti-aircraft guns. After the war, it was taken over by the port authority, and in 1984 it was sold to the Foundation for Listed Buildings for a symbolic 3 DKK, refurbished and opened to the public. There's a permanent historical exhibition in the casemate building, and you can go into the inner workings of the fort and see the parts that haven't been refurbished, but where dinners are still held from time to time. And when you need a break from traipsing around the fortress, you can visit the café and try their popular self-peel shrimp.

Address www.befaestningen.com | **Getting there** Boat departures from Langeliniekaj 5 (by the polar bear sculpture): May–June, Sat & Sun on the hour and half hour 10am–4.30pm; July–Aug, Tue–Sun on the hour and half hour 10am–4.30pm; Sept, Sat & Sun on the hour and half hour 10am–4.30pm. The boat leaves from the fortress at a quarter past and a quarter to, 10.15am–4.45pm. See cphwatershuttle.dk. | **Tip** You can walk from *The Little Mermaid* along the waterfront all the way to Nyhavn.

107 __ Trianglen

The first stop out of town

There's always a bustle of people, because Trianglen ('the Triangle') never sleeps. Although cars now dominate the scene, the triangular square really belongs to public transport and its passengers.

These days, buses convene here and drive off towards Nordhavn, Hellerup, Nørrebro or the City Centre, and the metro rushes away beneath the surface. But Trianglen has been a traffic junction for a long time before such modern inventions, back when first horse-drawn cabs and later clattering trams made their way around the city.

In the first half of the 19th century, Trianglen was outside the city walls and it was a nexus for Copenhageners who wished to take cabs to Northern Zealand. Perhaps they'd go to the Deer Park (Dyrehaven) in Klampenborg, where they could eat packed lunches, or – if they were more well-off – they could order lunch in one of the restaurants in the park or the Bakken amusement park.

Later on, Trianglen became a nexus for all of Østerbro, and many a tram had its final stop here. After the last stop of the evening, the trams would return to the depot on Blegdamsvej.

The old depot now houses the only indoor playground in Copenhagen, run by the City and free to use. It's a good place to take your kids on a rainy day, but do note that some mornings are reserved for children under the age of three.

Although the trams have gone, the old waiting room from 1907 remains in all its glory in the middle of the square. It's called Bien ('the Bee') and was designed by Peder Vilhelm Jensen-Klint. It's a listed building, and the round structure with its copper roof has become a landmark of inner Østerbro.

The name may be derived from the café that was run in the building for a number of years, when it was no longer used as a waiting room. The Bee is also colloquially known as 'the Tureen', because of the rounded roof with mythical animals on top – together they resemble the lid and handle of a soup tureen.

Address Trianglen, 2100 Copenhagen Ø | Getting there Bus 1A, 14 or Metro M 3 to Trianglen | Tip In the 17th century, the Vartov Redoubt stood at the site of Trianglen today. It was finished in 1630 and 30 years later – during the Swedish Wars of 1659 – played a part against the Swedish attack on Copenhagen (see ch. 83). The redoubt was abandoned after the Swedish Wars and there is no trace of it left.

108__ University of Copenhagen Main Building

Inspired by the colours of Pompeii

The gods Apollo and Athena are there to greet you as you enter – both in the form of statues made by H. V. Bissen (1798–1868) standing on either side of the broad staircase, and on many of the frescos on the walls.

The walls were painted by Georg Hilker (1807–1875) and Constantin Hansen (1798–1868) in the 1840s and 1850s and were modelled on Pompeii. French archaeologists had recently discovered that the ancient world was not just made of white marble, as had long been believed, and the colours of the newly-excavated mosaics and frescos from Pompeii were chosen for the university building, which boasts a multitude of shades, chiefly yellows, greens and blues.

It won't take you long to realise that all the paintings feature scenes from ancient history – there isn't a single Christian motif. This was a conscious – and controversial – decision. For centuries, the university had educated priests and clergymen, but was now increasingly focused on the new developments in archaeology and the natural sciences, and suddenly theology was pushed to the side. This was, of course, a controversial new direction at the time, but one that was maintained nonetheless.

If you're lucky, you'll be able to peek into the newly-renovated Great Hall, which is decorated with paintings depicting historical scenes related to the university, such as King Christian I receiving the Pope's permission to found the university, or students joining the fight during one of the many wars with Sweden. As you might suspect, these are somewhat idealised depictions of historical events. It's difficult to see, for instance, that the students were forced into battle in 1659, rather than being volunteers.

While you're in the Great Hall, don't forget to look in the adjacent Tapestry Room, containing six Flemish tapestries from the 1670s.

Address Frue Plads 4, 1168 Copenhagen K | **Getting there** Mon–Fri 9am–4pm | **Tip** In Fiolstræde (to the left of the university building, behind the cathedral) is the former Metropolitan School, which today belongs to the university. The building was designed by C. F. Hansen (see ch. 41) and is worth a look. It's open to the public during office hours.

109_ The University Gardens
Gardens for study, games and relaxation

'Wow, look – a waterfall!' says a little girl, to which her brother jadedly replies: 'I fell in there once.' The 'waterfall' is only about half a metre high, and the two children are spending a typical afternoon with their mother, walking around the University Gardens. This garden once belonged to the Royal Veterinary and Agricultural University, which now constitutes the University of Copenhagen Frederiksberg Campus.

For almost 150 years, the garden has kept its Romantic style with winding paths and a lovely lake with a very small island. The island is a big hit among young children who dare to go out to a narrow spit – it's completely safe, because there's a secure fence all the way out and on the island.

In addition to the old Veterinary Garden, the University Gardens include the Summer Flower Garden, the Rose Garden and the large open Green Garden in front of the former main building. The gardens have a variety of purposes, but first and foremost they serve as teaching and research areas for the campus, which houses students of forest and nature management and landscape architecture among others. The gardens are open to the public and have been ever since they were established in 1858, when they were part of the first modern campus in the country, inspired by a manor house, with stables, greenhouses and botanical collections. They were supposed to add to the pleasure of attending the university, and this is apparent from their goal of 'maintaining the structure and contents of the gardens to form a green context for study and work while inviting to relaxation and contemplation'.

So it's all a part of the plan for the University Gardens to be full of life, and it does seem like the students here spend more time outside than in other parts of the university. You can see them reading, having study group sessions and eating outside for most of the year, and all manner of games are played, from beer bowling to croquet.

Address Bülowsvej 17, 1870 Frederiksberg C, entrance through several gates on Bülowsvej and Thorvaldsensvej, www.plen.ku.dk/english/about/pfv/the-gardens | Getting there Bus 37 to Bülowsvej/Thorvaldsensvej | Hours Every day from dawn to dusk, except on 24 and 31 December | Tip Café Greenhouse in the Summer Flower Garden is run by students and they offer a student discount.

110 The Victorian Home

Be transported back to 1890

There's a time machine in Copenhagen. It costs 50 DKK to use, and it takes you back to 1890 for an hour. Tickets can be bought at the National Museum – either at the information desk or online – and you'll have a guide with you at all times.

The time machine is in a building on Frederiksholms Kanal, facing Christiansborg Castle. The building was bought by a merchant by the name of Rudolph Christensen (1849–1925) in the 1880s, at which point he was one of the wealthiest men in town. Between 1887 and 1890 he spared no expense when having the best craftsmen in town decorate the 300-square-metre, 16-room apartment for him and his family. As it would have been wildly inappropriate for Christensen to brag about his wealth, he showed it off in his home instead. There were stucco ceilings and woodcuttings on the panelling, hand-painted decorations instead of wallpaper, rugs and fashionable linoleum flooring, handmade furniture from the most expensive carpenter in the city, knick-knacks everywhere, and of course a decorated flush toilet. In addition, there was furniture and curtains adorned with numerous tassels (an exceedingly fashionable item at the time), and shortly after they moved in, they had a telephone and electrical lighting installed.

The home remains more or less unchanged from when the Christensen family moved there in 1890, with living and dining rooms, bedrooms, kitchen, bathroom and servants' quarters. It's quite unique to have a complete home preserved this way, and it's an interesting thing to see. Stating it mildly, the apartment is very far removed from the simplicity and clean lines of modern Scandinavian design. There is, however, no finer example of late 19th-century decorating.

Christensen's two daughters stayed in the apartment after their parents' deaths, and they chose not to change the interiors in any way. They died in 1963, bequeathing their home to the National Museum, allowing visitors to see this treasure.

Address Frederiksholms Kanal 18, 1220 Copenhagen K (there is no access to the building other than with a guide from the National Museum), www.en.natmus.dk/museums/the-victorian-home | **Getting there** Bus 2A, 23, 31, 37 to Stormbroen / Nationalmuseet | **Hours** The Victorian Home can only be seen on guided tours. The museum offers tours in English on Saturdays at 2pm (June – Sept). You can also ask to join a Danish-language tour, if you'd just like to see the interiors. | **Tip** If you need some fresh air after your visit, we recommend the Glyptotek's garden, not far from the museum.

111 War Graves in Vestre Cemetery

German refugees in Danish soil

There are rows and rows of crosses here in the southern end of Vestre Cemetery (Vestre Kirkegård). Beneath them lie 9,987 German soldiers and refugees – women and men, girls and boys. Their story is part of that of the Second World War and the occupation of Denmark.

In February 1945, the war was drawing to a close, as the Red Army marched through Eastern Europe on its way to Berlin. The German authorities forcefully evacuated 2 million Germans, mainly from East Prussia, and more than 200,000 of them wound up in occupied, but calm, Denmark. Many of them, especially infants and the elderly, died during their journey or shortly thereafter from exhaustion, malnutrition or disease. They are among those buried here.

When Denmark was liberated in May 1945, public sentiment was not favourable towards these German refugees, the result of five years of Nazi occupation. The mood was further soured by the fact that the refugees were staying in local schools and holiday camps, meaning that they were not open to Danish children. The refugees were seen as a provocation, not just politically and economically, but towards Danish national sentiment.

Nevertheless, these refugees stayed in Denmark under orders from the English, as neither they nor the other allied forces wanted to have to accommodate them in a devastated Germany under reconstruction.

The Germans were therefore interned in camps, partly to show the English that there was no room for them in Danish society, but also to protect them from the anger of the average Dane. The camps were harsh and rudimentary, but not inhumane, and the Danish government managed to lower mortality rates by securing proper healthcare and nutrition. The last refugee left Denmark in 1949.

Some 17,200 German refugees are buried in Denmark, most of them in Vestre Cemetery.

Address Vestre Cemetery, 2450 Copenhagen SV (take the entrance by Sydbanestien) | Getting there Bus 7A, 18 or S-train A, E to Sjælør | Hours Oct–Mar 7am–7pm, Apr–Sept 7am–10pm | Tip In Vestre Cemetery you can also see the graves of many famous Danes, such as the painter Vilhelm Hammershøi, polar explorer Knud Rasmussen, founder of the Danish labour movement Louis Pio, and several prime ministers.

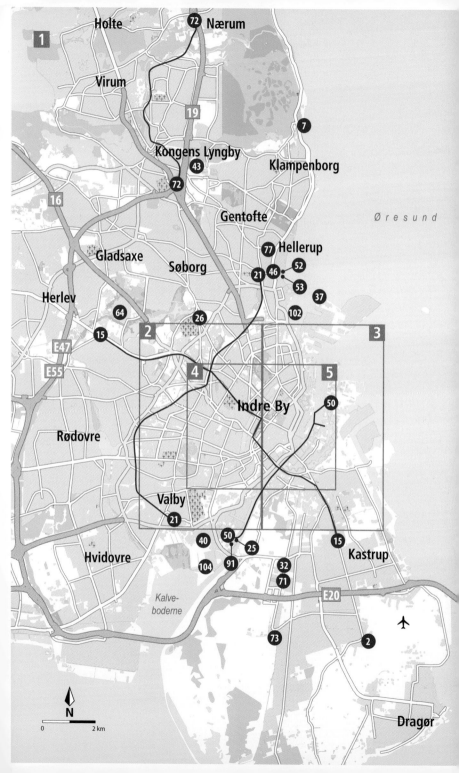

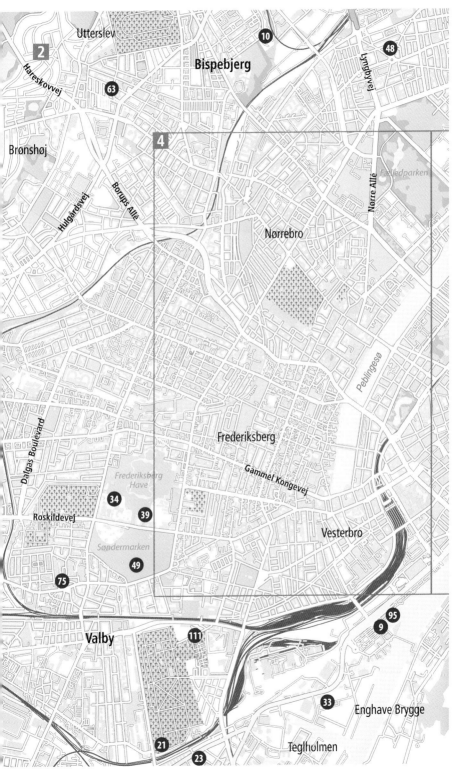

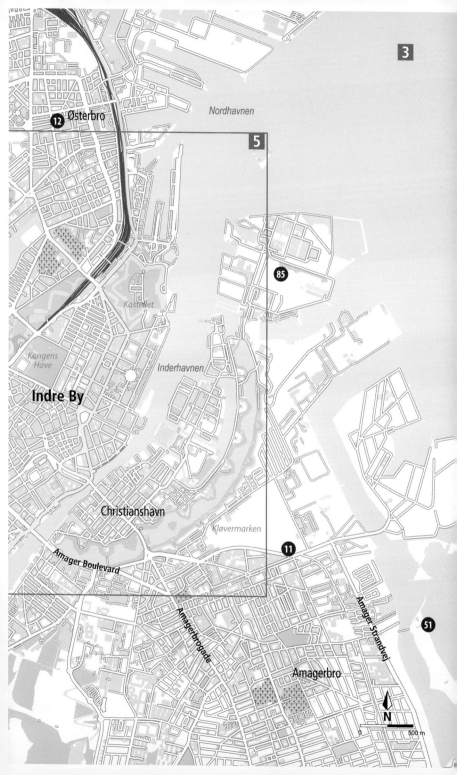

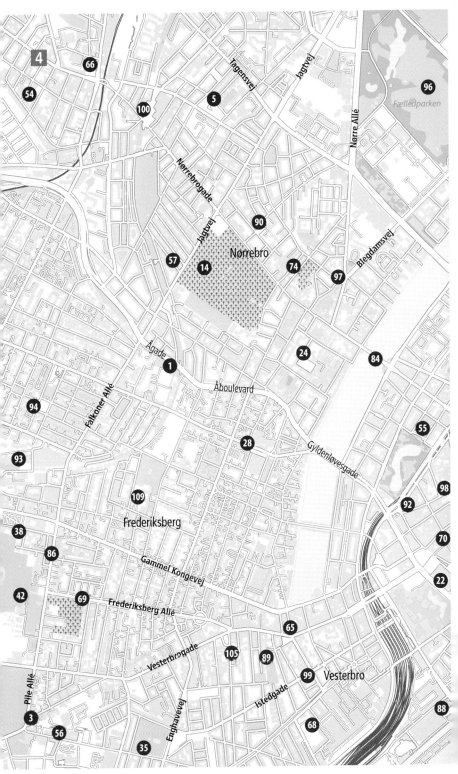

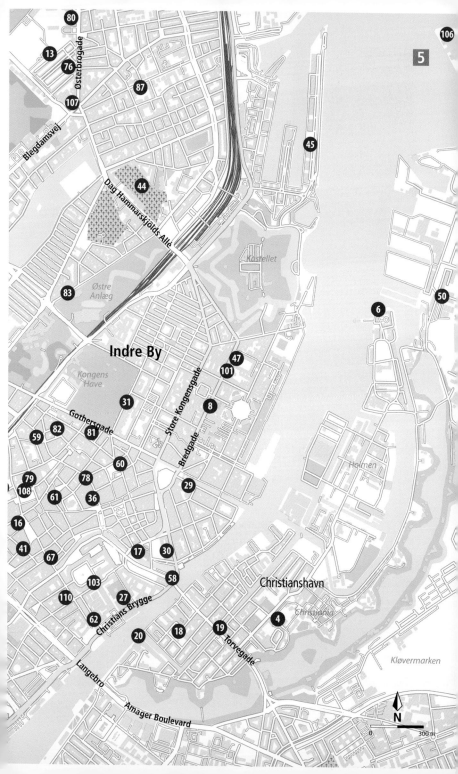

Maurizio Francesconi,
Alessandro Martini
111 Places in Turin
That You Shouldn't Miss
ISBN 978-3-7408-0414-5

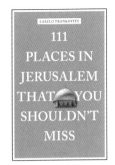

Laszlo Trankovits
111 Places in Jerusalem
That You Shouldn't Miss
ISBN 978-3-7408-0320-9

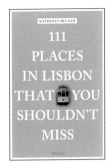

Kathleen Becker
111 Places in Lisbon
That You Shouldn't Miss
ISBN 978-3-7408-0383-4

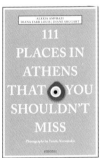

Alexia Amvrazi,
Diana Farr Louis, Diane Shugart,
Yannis Varouhakis
111 Places in Athens
That You Shouldn't Miss
ISBN 978-3-7408-0377-3

Alexandra Loske
111 Places in Brighton and
Lewes That You Shouldn't Miss
ISBN 978-3-7408-0255-4

Fabrizio Ardito
111 Places in Malta
That You Shouldn't Miss
ISBN 978-3-7408-0261-5

Tom Shields, Gillian Tait
111 Places in Glasgow
That You Shouldn't Miss
ISBN 978-3-7408-0256-1

Andrea Livnat,
Angelika Baumgartner
111 Places in Tel Aviv
That You Shouldn't Miss
ISBN 978-3-7408-0263-9

Kay Walter, Rüdiger Liedtke
111 Places in Brussels
That You Shouldn't Miss
ISBN 978-3-7408-0259-2

Thomas Fuchs
111 Places in Amsterdam
That You Shouldn't Miss
ISBN 978-3-7408-0023-9

Sybil Canac, Renée Grimaud,
Katia Thomas
111 Places in Paris
That You Shouldn't Miss
ISBN 978-3-7408-0159-5

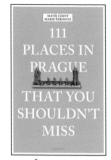

Matěj Černý, Marie Peřinová
111 Places in Prague
That You Shouldn't Miss
ISBN 978-3-7408-0144-1

Gillian Tait
111 Places in Edinburgh
That You Shouldn't Miss
ISBN 978-3-95451-883-8

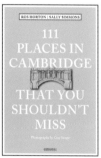

Rosalind Horton,
Sally Simmons, Guy Snape
111 Places in Cambridge
That You Shouldn't Miss
ISBN 978-3-7408-0147-2

Justin Postlethwaite
111 Places in Bath
That You Shouldn't Miss
ISBN 978-3-7408-0146-5

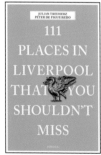

Julian Treuherz,
Peter de Figueiredo
111 Places in Liverpool
That You Shouldn't Miss
ISBN 978-3-95451-769-5

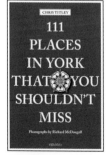

Chris Titley
111 Places in York
That You Shouldn't Miss
ISBN 978-3-95451-768-8

Frank McNally
111 Places in Dublin
That You Must Not Miss
ISBN 978-3-95451-649-0

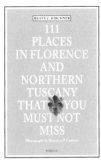

Beate C. Kirchner
**111 Places in Florence
and Northern Tuscany
That You Must Not Miss**
ISBN 978-3-95451-613-1

Christiane Bröcker,
Babette Schröder
**111 Places in Stockholm
That You Must Not Miss**
ISBN 978-3-95451-459-5

Marcus X. Schmid
**111 Places in Istanbul
That You Must Not Miss**
ISBN 978-3-95451-423-6

Annett Klingner
**111 Places in Rome
That You Must Not Miss**
ISBN 978-3-95451-469-4

Dirk Engelhardt
**111 Places in Barcelona
That You Must Not Miss**
ISBN 978-3-95451-353-6

John Sykes, Birgit Weber
**111 Places in London
That You Shouldn't Miss**
ISBN 978-3-95451-346-8

Peter Eickhoff
**111 Places in Vienna
That You Shouldn't Miss**
ISBN 978-3-95451-206-5

Lucia Jay von Seldeneck,
Carolin Huder
**111 Places in Berlin
That You Shouldn't Miss**
ISBN 978-3-7408-0589-0

Jo-Anne Elikann
**111 Places in New York
That You Must Not Miss**
ISBN 978-3-95451-052-8

The authors

Jan Gralle is a trained architect. He has worked as a freelance journalist specialising in urban culture, people and places. He was born and raised in Østerbro, and has since lived in the North-West neighbourhood, Albertslund, the City Centre and Nørrebro. He currently lives in Brønshøj.

Vibe Skytte has an MA in history, specialising in the history of Copenhagen. She was born and raised in Valby and has since lived in Frederiksberg, the City Centre, Sydhavnen and Vanløse.

The photographer

Kurt Rodahl Hoppe is a photographer and has illustrated a number of books about architecture and cultural history. He is a Copenhagener born and bred and currently lives in the City Centre.